TO THE FAMILIES

OF THOSE TIGERS

WHO WILL NEVER FLY AGAIN

# ACKNOWLEDGMENTS

I am grateful for the help given me in the preparation of this book by these members of the American Volunteer Group:

Harvey K. Greenlaw, Chief of Staff, second in command of the A.V.G.

Mrs. Olga Greenlaw, diarist and statistician of the A.V.G., who kept a daily report of activities which was published in the A.V.G. *NEWS*.

Charles R. Bond, Jr. of Dallas, Texas, Vice Commander of the First Squadron.

Henry Geselbracht of Glendale, California, Wing Man, Second Squadron.

Robert H. Neale of Seattle, Commander, First Squadron.

George T. Burgard of Sunbury, Pennsylvania, Flight Leader, First Squadron.

James T. Cross of Huntsville, Missouri, Flight Leader, First Squadron.

Hubert "Pat" Cavanah of Lakeland, Florida, Wing Man, Third Squadron.

Noel R. Bacon of Norfolk, Virginia, Flight Leader, Second Squadron.

Don Bernsdorf of Minneapolis, Wing Man, Second Squadron.

Lynn Hurst of Beaumont, Texas, Wing Man, Second Squadron.

Messrs. Greenlaw, Burgard, Cross, Bernsdorf, and Hurst have read all or a large part of the manuscript and have carefully checked facts and figures.

I am particularly indebted to George Kemp Fitch, who was in Burma during the winter of 1941-1942 for the Texas Company, for material on the battles and evacuation of Rangoon.

I wish also to thank the following for their valuable aid: Mr. H. R. Ekins, former Far Eastern correspondent of the United Press; Mr. Harry B. Price of China Defense Supplies, Inc.; Col. John H. Jouett, president of the Aeronautical Chamber of Commerce of the United States; Capt. Richard T. Aldworth, vice president of Central Aircraft Manufacturing Co., Federal, Inc. (CAMCO); the families and friends of the members of the American Volunteer Group; and members of the publicity staff of United China Relief in New York City.

# FOREWORD

It was Christmas Day, 1941, but the thoughts of the American people dwelt not on the glad old memory of Bethlehem but on the shocking facts of the new war in the Pacific and Asia. American soldiers were dying in the wilds of Luzon and Mindanao—dying in defeat. Pearl Harbor was a taste strong and bitter in every mouth. In Malaya and southeast Asia the Japanese juggernaut rode down all resistance. Along our own West Coast, in Alaska, and down at the Canal, ran the rumors and alarms of invasion. It was a sickening thing to see Americans doubting their own strength. It was staggering to think that Americans might have sound cause for doubt. On that day there was a kind of panic in the land.

Then suddenly, from far across the world, from a place that most Americans knew only as a name in an old Kipling song, came the news of the first shining victory over the forces of Nippon. The Flying Tigers had flown and struck.

The Flying Tigers? Who were they? The radio and the newspapers told us happily. They were American boys, from forty-one of our states, fighting pilots trained in our own Army and Navy; and now members of the new American Volunteer Group employed by the Government of Generalissimo Chiang Kai-shek to protect the lifeline of China, the Burma Road.

On Christmas Day a Japanese aerial Armada had headed for Rangoon, the seaport of Burma. There, awaiting transport to China, crowding the wharves and warehouses, were many millions of American dollars' worth of lend-lease supplies and material. The Jap raiders came in bold confidence born of their easy triumphs throughout the Pacific. They came in the knowledge that their enemies had mustered only a skeleton air force for the defense of Burma, an air force of a few dozen planes and men without replacements and with scant supplies of fuel and ammunition. Nevertheless, they came in strength, in

7

two waves, seventy bombers escorted by thirty-eight fighting planes in all, to blast Rangoon out of the war.

As the first bombardier studied his sight for the first blow, four little fighting ships raced down out of the sun onto the backs of the invaders. Joined by their fourteen comrades, the defenders raged through the sky, and soon eleven Japanese pursuits and eight bombers had fallen flaming into the rivers and rice fields below. At least nine more crashed before the main Jap force scattered and fled from those strange and terrible fighters of Burma that wore the face of the shark on their noses and the little cartoon figures along their sides. The Flying Tigers went back to their airdrome near the banyan trees. They had made their bow to history.

Their brilliant defense of Rangoon that day did more than give the air force of the Imperial Japanese Army cause for reconsideration. It gave the Chinese their first great aerial victory in over four years of war. It lifted the gloom of defeats and doubtings from the American mind. And it sent a thrill of pride and a chill of determination right where they could do the most good—down the great American spine. Those were the Christmas gifts of the Tigers to the folks back home.

They went on from there. They went on in smoke and flame and blood and death to compose their epic—the most spectacular in the annals of air warfare. They saved Rangoon and the Burma Road for sixty-five precious days. They became the demigods of fighting China. To Madame Chiang Kai-shek they were "my angels—with or without wings." This is their story.

RUSSELL WHELAN

# CHAPTER ONE

The strangest venture of the Second World War—the venture of the American Volunteer Group, which sent two hundred and fifty American boys to China long before December 7, 1941—was the upshot of a series of critical events in Asia.

The story begins with Chiang Kai-shek, the great lieutenant of the little doctor, Sun Yat-sen, who had guided the revolution of 1911 that overthrew the imperial Manchu throne and gave the people of China their chance for freedom and the pursuit of happiness.

Ironically, Chiang had learned the art of the soldier in the Tokyo Military Academy, and served for a time in the 13th Field Artillery of the Imperial Japanese Army. In 1908, a youth of twenty, he returned to China to work for its liberation from the Manchu rule. After the revolution came the long years of civil war, with Chiang emerging in 1927 as the leader of the Kuomintang Party and the general of its small but well-trained army. His dream was the unification and modernization of his country. The sprawling land of China was disunited by the enmities of civil war, by age-long sectionalisms, by difference in language, and by lack of inter-communication among the provinces. Opposed to Chiang were the Communists, a growing power in the rural districts; the provincial governors, jealous of the almost absolute power they had even in the days of the Manchus; and the war-lords, those bizarre brigands who gouged the little people at every turn and only accidentally served their country when they killed each other off.

Chiang actually had to conquer China in order to save it. Much of this conquest he achieved in the field, in one bitter campaign after another. But some of his opponents were strong, and Chiang's army was small, which left diplomacy as the only winning weapon. He had to be a Talleyrand and a Napoleon all in one. And even when he succeeded in establishing a semblance of authority over the various factions, he had still to awaken the somnolent and illiterate peasantry to the necessity of a strong China. He knew that the strength of his government must, in the end, rest with the people. But the Chinese traditionally, and by choice, look backward, and Chiang's preachments were all of the burning present and the ominous future. With the courage of the toughened campaigner that he was, he assaulted that great wall of inertia which four hundred and fifty millions of his countrymen had raised against the modern world. He knew his time was short and he worked strenuously, almost frantically, to prepare for that day when Japan would draw the dagger it had fingered so long.

Long before 1930 he had made sizable breeches in that wall. Modern schools and colleges and modern industries were firmly established in all the great cities of eastern China. The country was well on its way to a place in the sun among the nations, and no one saw it so clearly as the militarists of Japan, and their sponsors, the capitalists. These worthies wanted China to continue as their own private preserve, with its fruits to be plucked at their leisure.

When China began to emerge from the cocoon of the centuries (energetically propelled by Chiang Kai-shek) the Japanese decided to strike before it was too late. In 1931 they attacked and occupied the Chinese provinces of Manchuria. In 1932 they attacked Shanghai and after two months of bitter fighting occupied most of the Chinese areas there. After consolidating their conquest of Manchuria and draining that rich land of much of its wealth, they moved into Charhar and Jehol. Finally in 1937, when they had put down all pacifist opposition at home, the Japanese military machine struck at the heart of China.

The shots fired upon the Chinese at the Marco Polo Bridge outside Peiping on July 7, 1937, were shots that should have been heard " 'round the world." They announced the war to dominate Asia and the Pacific. But they went unheeded in a Europe and an America content in the fool's paradise of peace at any price.

In 1930, as we have seen, the re-born China of Chiang Kai-shek realized that an attack by Japan was inevitable. The question was how to defend against it? China had

10

neither the money nor the materials and crafts to build a navy capable of challenging the ambitions of Tokyo. It had the manpower for a large army, but lacked the industries to equip this manpower for modern war. Chiang felt, however, that a strong air force was a practical possibility. Accordingly, after the invasion of Manchuria, he asked the British Government to install a military aviation system for China. The British declined, on the ground that such a move might be frowned on in Tokyo. Chiang then turned to the United States Government, which agreed, after considerable parley, to send an "un-official" mission to China.

In 1932 this American air mission arrived in Hangchow under the leadership of Col. John H. Jouett,* who had recently retired from the U.S. Army Air Forces. Jouett, a pioneer in American military aviation, was a disciple of the late General "Billy" Mitchell, the great prophet of air power who suffered so long without the honors that developments of the Second World War would finally heap upon his name. With Jouett came nine experienced U.S. Army pilots, among them Christy Mathewson, Jr., son of the famous old pitcher of the New York Giants, and Harvey Greenlaw, who later was to become second in command of the American Volunteer Group.

At Hangchow Jouett found a couple of dilapidated hangars, a small and bumpy airfield, and an assortment of Russian and British airplanes so old and badly cared for that they offered a greater threat to China than to a potential invader. He learned that the Chinese regarded military aviation as a profession reserved for the élite of money, family, or political power. But he met there the man named Chiang Kai-shek, who could listen, and understand. Chiang gave Jouett a free hand for his plan to build in Hangchow a "Randolph Field" for China. Jouett promptly fired eighty-five per cent of the pilots in the Chinese Air Force, demoted every officer two ranks, and raised the pay of all fliers from $30 Chinese to $100 Chinese per month

*Now President of the Aeronautical Chamber of Commerce of the United States. While at West Point, Jouett played end against Knute Rockne of Notre Dame in the famous 35 to 13 game in 1913 which introduced the East to the art and mystery of the forward pass in football.

11

to improve morale and protect against "squeeze," the Oriental term for graft. Six weeks later the Central Chinese Aviation Academy was established with steel hangars and facilities for two hundred men. A year later it had two hundred and fifty modern fighting ships and three hundred and fifty Chinese pilots trained to the exacting standards of the U.S. Army, the highest in the world.

But Japan didn't like all this, and used diplomatic pressure to force Jouett's mission out of China. Regretfully Chiang had to accede to Tokyo's demand in December 1934, and for a time thereafter China's air power came under the direction of various soldiers of fortune, Russian, British, Italian, and American, many of these last enlisted through the efforts of Dr. Margaret "Mom" Chung, the Chinese woman surgeon of San Francisco.

In the spring of 1937, with the Japanese now firmly established in Manchuria and their menace to China steadily mounting, Chiang was confronted with the almost complete collapse and demoralization of his air force. To signify the importance which he attached to the aerial arm, he placed his wife, Madame Chiang Kai-shek (Mei-ling Soong) in nominal command, while his agents searched the world for a leader. This search at last plucked Claire L. Chennault from his little home town with the unique name of Waterproof, in Louisiana. There Chennault was living with his wife and eight children following his retirement (for partial deafness) from the U.S. Army Air Corps. His book *The Role of Pursuit Aviation,* which outlined his theories for the employment of swift fighting planes against bombardment from the air, had brought him some notice in aviation circles. He had been a nine days' wonder as an acrobatic pilot when he organized a tour of the United States with two other army fliers billed as "Three Men on a Flying Trapeze." Many thousands of onlookers at aviation exhibitions had opened wide their eyes and mouths as Chennault and his partners performed intricate stunt and formation flying in unison while their three planes were tied together by short lengths of rope. So he had known a little fame—not much—and now at forty-seven, afflicted with the deafness which is so often the occupational disability of the aviator, he longed for the activity which he loved but which his country's army denied him. China! And a war!

Perhaps he would find on the other side of the world the opportunity to practice his theories of sky fighting. Claire L. Chennault, burning with ambition and desire, packed his duffel and was off for China.

There he inherited a grab-bag of adventuresome young men known as the "Foreign Legion." About one half of this romantic assortment, he quickly discovered, were fancy liars with little or no previous experience in military aviation. With a few good men as a nucleus—notably his partners of the "Flying Trapeze" days, W. C. McDonald and J. H. Williamson, who had recommended him to Chiang—Chennault strove mightily to give China overnight a semblance of air defense against the Japanese onslaught. His planes were few, but good and modern, bought at great cost to China from Europe and America. But "overnight" was not long enough, and in bitter violation of his own judgment, he had to entrust these fine new ships to some of his misfit force. The inevitable happened. His visiting firemen of the air promptly cracked up eleven of twenty-two Vultee and Gladiator fighters while essaying the rather elementary task of landing them on the field at Hangchow. They also destroyed four new Martin bombers the same way. And soon after that, when the Japanese came over in force, the legionnaires scrambled into the cockpits of the remaining planes and took off in all directions at once, by which maneuver they quickly demolished the only surviving Martin and fifteen additional fighters. The Japs, far overhead, must have been puzzled indeed by this self-slaughter of the innocents.

What this travesty, piled upon a long series of similar didos, must have meant to Claire Chennault is pretty obvious. Here he was, a scientist of sky warfare, a peak product of the great training system of the U.S. Army Air Forces, set down in China to build a modern air force —and lacking all the essential ingredients for the job —men, money, planes. He didn't have them. He couldn't get them. About all he had achieved in three years of work was the knowledge, carefully gathered and treasured, of how to lick the Japanese air force if ever he should have those men, those planes, and that money. The chances of getting them seemed as remote as the moon.

The Japanese spread their conquest of eastern and

northern China without serious interruption for two years, driving Chiang's government from its capital of Nanking and subsequently from the provisional capital at Hankow. The government was now established deep in the hinterland, at Chungking, and every day throughout the "bombing season" (April to October) the big Jap ships would be reported on the way by the radio alarm system Chennault had established. He would know exactly how many bombers were coming, where they were from minute to minute, and how many fighter escorts accompanied them, if any. Usually there were no fighters, because the Japs knew well they would meet no resistance. The alarms would sound, and the people of Chungking, the city built on and around a mountain, would scurry into the caves they had dug in their cliffs, and wait for the terror. It rarely failed them. Once four thousand were killed when bombs exploded simultaneously at either end of the largest tunnel. Chennault, witnessing this indignity of undisputed bombing, writhed with the anguish of a man who knows his trade but cannot obtain the tools to practice it. Behind him were years of striving, of turmoil, of disappointment, and defeat. Confronting him, punctuated by each blast of the bombs, was the galling failure of Claire Chennault's personal air mission to China.

The future? Well, he was determined that there would be no more snatching at the straws of futility. When harassed military leaders and nervous statesmen cried for wholesale purchases of military planes to halt this continual insult of the bombs, Chennault argued against a repetition of the old mistakes. Even if airplanes could be brought to China by the thousands—which they could not in the world of 1940—they would offer no answer to the problem, he insisted. What China needed for its aerial defense, he said, was a pool of thousands of expert combat fliers, a few thousand modern fighting planes, supported by a trained ground organization—the whole under a unified command. Chennault must have thought of his old friend General "Billy" Mitchell when he outlined this impossible program; impossible, not alone because of China's poverty in money and in aviators, but because the previous sources of supply, Britain, Russia, and the United States, were now concentrating all their military plane production on the task of stopping Adolf Hitler in Europe.

Chennault's opposition to half measures was shared by the Generalissimo and by that titan of finance and industry, Dr. T. V. Soong, head of the Bank of China, brother of the renowned Soong sisters, and hence, brother-in-law of Chiang Kai-shek and of the mourned father of the revolution, Sun Yat-sen. With bitter regret they resigned the skies of China to Japan, and the bombs continued to fall on the cities and towns all through 1940. And then, in 1941, came the new crisis of the Burma Road; and with it, the golden opportunity for Claire Chennault of Waterproof, Louisiana.

# CHAPTER TWO

*The Burma Road is China's jugular vein.*—LIN YU-TANG

An air traveler over southwest China in the fall of 1937 looked down upon that gray wilderness and was surprised to see many thousands of moving figures along the mountainsides and in the deep gorges. He asked his pilot what they were.

"They're the people of China," the pilot replied. "There's a couple hundred thousand of 'em strung out all through here, trying to build a road. A road through that country! Just take a look at it, will you? Some of the steepest mountains on earth, and malaria darn near every foot of the way. Yes, and the poor devils haven't even got steel pickaxes, let alone stone crushers and steam rollers. Well, you and I can see it's impossible, but I wouldn't bet on it. This is China, you know."

The traveler knew. He had seen the Great Wall, built by the forefathers of these same people many centuries before, against another invader. Now below him he saw the people of the new China launching another miracle of human ingenuity and endurance for the salvation of their country. They had lost their access to the Pacific through Japanese occupation and blockade. So they were building a road toward the Indian Ocean. These people, he thought, would build a road to the Atlantic if necessity demanded. They were that kind of people.

Between the ranges of the mountains in Yunnan Province lay some of the deepest canyons in the world—the canyons of the Mekong and Salween rivers. To fashion a highway over that wild terrain would have been an immense challenge to the best in modern engineering intelligence and machinery. The Chinese had neither of these; and even manpower, for once in China's history, was a problem. The population of Yunnan was small and weakened by the old curse of malaria. So the Government

16

of Free China had called upon men and women of every town and village within eight days' foot journey from the road. They came, with their children, their primitive tools, and even their food supplies. They removed the debris of the cliff sides with handmade baskets. They smoothed the road with stone rollers which they carved out of the rock and hitched to bullocks; or, lacking bullocks, to a train of their own bodies. They worked, and they died at their work by the uncounted thousands, through the raw winter and the searing heat of summer, through landslides, floods, and plague. They dug two thousand culverts and built three hundred bridges, including two suspension bridges across the gorges. For seven hundred and twenty-six miles they cut a level strip from nine to twenty feet in width across the rocky face of Asia. They built the most dramatic, the most important highway, in the history of the world. They built the Burma Road.

An American engineer expressed the marvel of it when he said: "My God, they scratched this thing out of the mountains with their finger-nails."

They scratched it out of the mountains because their Generalissimo had foreseen that a road southward to the sea might one day be essential to China's fight for its life.

The obvious first moves of the Japanese conquest, back in 1937 and 1938, had been the seizure of the seaports to choke off supplies from abroad; and the occupation of the eastern cities to strangle the domestic industrial life of China. Chiang anticipated all this. He knew that Russia, nervously building up its own armaments, would send him only a trickle of supplies across the old caravan route to the northwest. He needed the sea. He could still reach the sea through French Indo-China via the railroad, but he foresaw that Japanese blockade, plus possible Japanese occupation there, would close him off sooner or later. So he looked far to the south, where the Burmese city of Rangoon touched the Indian Ocean. A railroad ran from Rangoon northward to Lashio in Burma. If a highway could be built across the mountains of his own province of Yunnan, from its capital, Kunming, to reach that railhead at Lashio—? Well, China might still evade the death grip of Japan.

He gave the order. Construction of the Burma Road

began in the late summer of 1937. Sixteen months later the first motor trucks from Lashio, laden with guns and gasoline from the wharves of Rangoon, roared into the city of Kunming. The Chinese celebrated this opening of their second road to the sea. And even when the Japanese began their almost daily bombings of the new highway, the Chinese accepted the fresh complication with true philosophy.

"Let them come," they said. "It costs the Japanese a thousand dollars every time they drop a bomb on the road. Even when they hit it, we can fill up the holes for only a few cents' worth of labor. So, if they bomb it often enough, Japan will soon be broke."

But when France collapsed before the Germans in 1940, power politics succeeded where the bombs had failed. Britain, its spirit stricken by the loss of its ally, and uncertain of American support, yielded to Tokyo's demand that the road through Burma be closed. This was a major triumph for the Japanese and a staggering blow to China. Staggering, because there was still the railroad through Indo-China to the sea, over which came the great preponderance of the tools of war.

Japan swiftly delivered the knockout. It notified the French authorities in Indo-China that continuation of rail transport into China would constitute an unfriendly act. The colonial French, orphaned by the fall of their motherland, yielded to the pressure.

That was the darkest day in modern China's history. The claws of Japan tightened about her neck. The appeasers and the traitors assured the people that peace at any price was a golden treasure. Even the great Chiang must have felt that his dream might now be lost. For three months his people suffered and despaired behind the total blockade. But Chiang, characteristically, did not wait upon Fate. He rallied his armies to new heights of resistance. He sent some of the highest officials of his government to Washington and London to present his case—that help to China would prove sound insurance for the future of their own interests in Asia.

These missions were not immediately successful, because the march of Hitler through Europe then riveted the attention of the two English-speaking powers. But at last Winston Churchill reached an understanding with Franklin

D. Roosevelt to the effect that a firm gesture toward Japan was in order. The British ordered the road through Burma reopened.

China received this announcement with boundless rejoicing. The first trucks that rumbled across the Burmese border into China were greeted as heavenly chariots of deliverance. But soon the cold dank fact seeped into China's consciousness—the Burma Road was almost useless as a channel of supply. The statistics told the story. In that winter of 1940-1941 the Burma transport averaged only about four thousand tons a month, whereas the lost rail line through Indo-China had delivered close to forty thousand tons. Again there were no machines for the factories, no oil and gasoline for the trucks, no shells for the guns, no medicines for the sick and wounded.

Deceived, disappointed, starved for supply, China fought on while its leaders tackled the agonizing problems of the Burma Road. The bottlenecks were not all physical and geographical. Incredible stupidity, chicanery, and ineptitude contributed their share. That is a long and separate story.

But in the early fall of 1941, when the monthly transport rose as high as thirty thousand tons as a result of the system installed by an American commission of transportation experts, the Burma Road at last became what it was intended to be—the lifeline of fighting China. It was not all that the Chinese would have wanted, but it was all they had beyond the smuggling routes through the Japanese lines to the China Sea. The Burma Road now gave Chiang's armies some of the materials they required. These precious shipments had to be protected from Japanese bombs, as did the Road itself. What China needed for this vital task was a defensive air force of the best modern type. Strangely, deviously, dramatically, China got what it needed.

# CHAPTER THREE

America in the winter of 1941 was emerging from behind the blindfold fastened on its eyes by years of peace, of wishful thinking, and isolationist oratory. It was thinking about its own safety and conjecturing how to ensure that safety. Slowly the public—and the politicians—were coming to suspect that our stake in Asia might be even more important to us than the boon of peace itself. From Asia came the rubber, the tin, the manganese, the antimony, the hemp and jute and shellac, the quinine and strychnine, and other essentials of our civilization. Japan, with its announced policy of "Asia for the Asiatics," easily interpreted by the dullest-witted as meaning "Asia for Japan," threatened to cut off our access to these articles.

Also, some were coming to realize that in a strong and unified China lay the best hope for peace in Asia; and for a permanent check to the threat of the military jingoists of Japan.

For a long time before this, Chinese spokesmen in Washington had been laboring the point that America's own lifeline in Asia lay athwart the path of empire Japan had mapped for itself. But the gigantic bogey of Hitlerism and the fear of involvement in war dominated official thought.

With evident half-heartedness, our government had applied what are known as economic sanctions to deprive Japan of some of the sinews of war. We renounced our trade treaty and cut down, little by little, our shipments of scrap iron (bomb fragments to the Chinese), airplanes and parts, machine tools, and the high octane gasoline that drove the Jap bombers over the defenseless cities of China. Over many months we continued to slap Japan smartly on the wrist with such devices, which did nothing to benefit the Chinese or to dissuade Japan from its plans and purposes. Indeed they were even more infuriating to the Chinese than to the Japs, being tentative half-measures that illustrated our lack of any well-defined policy for Asia and the Pacific.

And the "made in America" scrap iron continued to murder the helpless men, women, and children of China.

Then the Japanese invaded Indo-China, and we began to see the Rising Sun for what it was—the Oriental version of the Swastika, impure and not very simple. Where eloquence and logic had failed, the pressures of actuality succeeded. Dr. T. V. Soong, in Washington armed with authority as Minister for Foreign Affairs of the Republic of China, at last had history on his side to support his arguments. Immediately, American help for China went into the works. On March 15, 1941, President Franklin D. Roosevelt announced a policy of "all-out" aid to China through the medium of lend-lease.

The policy was splendid news to "T. V." and his people, but the quality of its execution depended on the industrial system of America, already working overtime to meet the frantic demands of Britain and the necessity of building up our own armaments. Nevertheless the crucial importance of the Burma Road in the battle for the world could not be overlooked. Shiploads of guns and trucks and gasoline and all the myriad items necessary for waging war were soon pointing for Rangoon and the long journey northward. Many millions of American dollars were paying for those cargoes. They had to be delivered into the hands of the Chinese, and "T. V." prescribed to the White House a method for ensuring that overland delivery from Rangoon.

The prescription called for an air force of the best military planes obtainable, manned by the best available American pilots under the command of the best tactician of military aviation in Asia, Col. Claire L. Chennault of the Chinese Army. It was a daring prescription for a desperate case. There were complications galore. The United States was nominally at peace with Japan. The Neutrality Act, an experiment in statecraft noble in motive, but now beginning to rip sadly at the seams under the stresses of a world at war, forbade several practices which now were urgent needs. Fortunately, "T. V.," a realist himself, was dealing with realists. The prescription for the Burma Road was filled.

One hundred pursuit planes (P-40's) were in their crates at the Curtiss Wright Airplane Company factories in

Buffalo. The British Purchasing Commission had already rejected them as "obsolescent" for European service against the Luftwaffe. They were consigned to China, to be paid for out of one of the four loans, totalling $150,000,000 which Dr. Soong had arranged for on the security of tungsten, tin, and tung oil exports to the United States.

Who would fly the Tomahawks over the Burma Road? Chennault, newly made a brigadier general of the Chinese Army, arrived in Washington early in 1940. Chennault and Dr. Soong proposed that a volunteer air force of pilots and ground crew members and radio technicians be recruited in the United States, to serve as a completely integrated and independent unit of the Chinese Army. "T. V." and Chennault had seen too many catastrophic disappointments result from the soldier-of-fortune type of air force. Time was now of the essence. What they needed, and what they asked for, was a force of pilots trained to the rigid standards of the United States Army and Navy, who, with very little additional instruction, could handle expertly any type of fighting aircraft that might be obtained for China.

The actual enlistment of the men of the American Volunteer Group was assigned to a company formed for the purpose by William D. Pawley, an American who had operated airplane factories in China for several years. This company, called Central Aircraft Manufacturing Company, Federal, Inc., or CAMCO for short, opened offices in Rockefeller Center in New York City to handle all the business of A.V.G. personnel. Chennault decided to superintend the initial enlistments himself, and then hand the job over to other veteran flying officers whose judgment he could trust to fill his specifications for the ideal combat flier. He wanted men not younger than twenty-two, nor older than twenty-eight, with at least two years of training as pilots in our Army, Navy, or Marine Corps; men disciplined to military life but possessing initiative and the qualities of leadership. The requirements of courage and the love of a fight went without saying; but no break-neck harum scarums. He wanted professional soldiers—soldiers of the air.

So it happened that during May, June, and July 1941 the commanding officers of various American Army air fields and Naval air training stations summoned some of the best of their young fliers to confidential meetings behind closed doors. There the youngsters looked upon a man most of them had known before only as a name on a textbook called *The Role of Pursuit Aviation*. A few, as awestruck kids, had looked into the skies and marveled at the wondrous antics of "Three Men on a Flying Trapeze." But here he was in person, Claire L. Chennault, of Waterproof, Hangchow, Chungking, and way stations, a leather-faced, steel-eyed, wiry man of fifty-one with the aura of adventure and hardship unmistakably about him. They listened to Chennault.

It was no chore for him to give them his message. He knew, because the highest authority in the land had ordered it, that he was addressing some of the best-trained military pilots in this country. With them he was in his element, among his own kind, who spoke his own tongue and would understand his words.

He told them, in his terse clipped manner, the whole story of China and the Burma Road as he saw it. He explained that he wanted to enlist fliers for a brand new type of military organization, to be known as the American Volunteer Group, which would work as a unit of the Chinese Army Air Force from its own bases in Burma and southeastern China to protect shipments over the Road. Their commander would be himself, Claire L. Chennault. One year contracts with CAMCO, as agent for the Chinese Government, would govern their service. They would retain their United States citizenship, and at the expiration of their contracts they might be reinducted into the service of their choice without loss of rank. In the event of war involving the United States of America, they had the privilege of resigning at once. They would have the best military airplanes that the exigencies of the times might make available; already one hundred Curtiss P-40 pursuit ships (Tomahawks), the plane some of them knew well, had been acquired. The initial personnel would comprise about one hundred pilots, and some one hundred and fifty others for ground crew, medical services, and administration. This force would be augmented as additional men, machines, and shipping accommodations could be obtained.

Chennault stressed the necessity for secrecy, pointing out the ticklish international situation and the fact that this nation was at peace with Japan. He did not wave the flag, but he did tell them that America was undoubtedly heading into a war of its own, where it would urgently need fliers with actual combat experience. Their experience in China would equip them, as nothing else could, to teach the intricacies of modern sky fighting to the fledgling eagles of the United States. He did not need to tell them what they already knew, that any blows they could strike home at "friendly" Japan would in effect be blows delivered in the defense of their own country.

After his statement of the preliminaries, Chennault invariably found more than half his listeners eager to enlist with the A.V.G. then and there. He practically had to hold them off while he outlined the details:

Pilots would receive salaries of $600 American a month from the date of enlistment, with $675 a month for flight leaders and $750 a month for squadron commanders. For each Japanese plane destroyed, the Chinese Government guaranteed, upon presentation of proof, to pay a bonus of $500. Ground crew members would receive salaries ranging from $150 to $350 a month, depending on experience and qualifications. The entire personnel would be established in accommodations as nearly approaching their customary mode of life as it was possible to achieve in Burma and China.

The actual one-year contract submitted to them by CAMCO as secret agent for the Chinese Government was a masterpiece of evasion. According to this document they were to engage only in the manufacture, operation, and repair of airplanes, not in their destruction. But Chennault supplied the facts the contract omitted. They were being asked to fight a war. This was no picnic. Japan had a strong air force, he said, and every man in it would be anxious to kill them. The Japs would out-number them, and they must never underestimate Japanese air power, the efficiency of its planes, and the skill of its pilots.

Enlistments were now in order. Many of these young fellows were burning with desire to practice their dangerous craft. There was one lad, though, who struck a false note, and on striking it, was stricken from the lists. He merely rose to inquire whether the A.V.G. would be fighting its end of the war on the basis of an eight hour day and a five day week. Chennault said No.

Each applicant was scrutinized carefully in personal interviews and through check of family and service background. Chennault, well pleased with the caliber of the men and the enthusiasm they were showing for the job, flew to Burma to arrange for the training and living accommodations of the A.V.G. He left the bulk of the enlistment job to Captain Harry C. Claiborne of the U.S. Army Air Corps, to C. B. "Skip" Adair, an ex-Army pilot and an old China "hand" with Chennault, and Captain Richard T. Aldworth, a veteran pilot of the First World War, now vice-president of CAMCO. These men soon settled on ninety pilots and one hundred and fifty mechanics and technicians for the first expeditionary force of the A.V.G. A similar number were signed up for the second expedition, scheduled for December.

The chosen men were sworn to secrecy and told to stand by for further orders. In mid-summer and fall they received telegrams ordering them to report at a hotel in San Francisco, individually and with closed mouths. There was no wish to arouse the curiosity of any foreign agents with the sight of so many tanned and muscular young men with an identical gleam in their eyes—the gleam of high adventure. They arrived, from the naval air training stations at San Diego, Norfolk, and Pensacola and the army's MacDill, Brooks, Kelly, Chanute and Mitchel fields, from airplane carriers and Marine squadrons, a typical American assortment of names and racial strains. There was a flier from Princeton and a flier from Cicero. There were boys from the Bronx and boys from Walla Walla, Seekonk, and Scarsdale. There was a Gallagher, a Petach, a Dupuoy, a Jernstedt, a Jones and a couple of Smiths. There were two young women volunteer nurses: Emma Jane Foster, a Penn State college graduate, and Josephine Stewart of Dallas, Texas. They were to become two of the most popular girls in human history.

About one half of the pilots were Navy-trained, six came from the U.S. Marine Flying Corps, and thirty-five had served with the U.S. Army Air Forces.

In lots of twenty to forty they went aboard Dutch ships,

listed as tourists, business men, acrobats, artists, embalmers, vaudeville actors, and everything else but what they were, soldiers hired to fight a nation at peace with their own in a land ten thousand miles away. The Dutch ships of the Java-Pacific Line traveled "blacked out," but barkeepers the world over will listen to reason. During those days the boys had a wonderful time unleashing their voracious young appetites upon the five-meal-a-day cuisine of the Dutch steamers. Older heads tried to institute a routine of daily calisthenics lest the argonauts arrive at their destination too fat to enter a Tomahawk without a derrick attachment; but the boys declined to engage in any muscular activity more strenuous than swallowing. They had a lovely, noisy trip.

The ships first visited Honolulu, Manila and Batavia, cities that would soon know the full fury of the war, and then from Singapore made the long journey to Rangoon, the capital of the then British province of Burma, which was to be the scene of their most amazing exploits. They sailed up the Rangoon River twenty-one miles, marveling at the great golden dome of the Shwe Dagon pagoda, shimmering in the sunlight, and consulting their guidebooks for identification of this new wonder. It was September 1941, when the first members of the A.V.G. disembarked at Rangoon, some in civilian clothes, and some wearing plain khaki uniforms with no insignia. As their ship approached the city they were vividly reminded of their mission by the scene along the three-mile length of wharves, where storage yards and warehouses bulged with thousands of packing cases awaiting shipment by rail and road to the north. This was American lend-lease material, the lifeblood of fighting China.

They found upon inquiry that many of the packing cases had been standing there for weeks and months, while China clamored for the supplies, and clamored in vain. One of the reasons for this, they learned, was the British custom ruling that permitted clearance of any article only when every one of its kind mentioned in the bill of lading was present on the spot and accounted for. Hence, if the papers described a shipment of five thousand automobile truck tires, and ten of these were mislaid during an unloading, the other four thousand nine hundred and ninety gathered dust on the wharves until the missing ten turned up. If they remained missing, the four thousand nine hundred and ninety stayed where they were, thus serving the ends of red tape but not of nations and empires fighting for their lives.

The travelers were permitted little time to see the sights and sense the amazing variety of smells that distinguished the hybrid city of Rangoon—a city nominally Burmese, where Indians held most of the jobs, where the Chinese operated the stores, and the British ruled over all. Chennault was waiting at Toungoo, and they set off over the rickety railroad for the north.

On one trip two of the ground crew lads disappeared, but were shortly discovered to be relieving the monotony of travel by chasing each other along the tops of the coaches. The train staff at last joined in the game and cornered the miscreants at the risk of life, limb, and dignity.

At Toungoo they occupied barracks of the British at Kyedaw Airdrome ten miles outside the town. Only a few of the Tomahawks had been assembled at Rangoon and flown to Toungoo when the first batch of A.V.G. men arrived there, so they had opportunities to get acquainted with the British soldiers stationed near by, and with the countryside.

For most members of the A.V.G. it was their first trip outside the United States. Any enthusiasm they might have held for foreign parts was speedily liquidated by the hot and humid realities of life in Burma, the country of steamy jungles, where rain falls almost constantly from June through September; the land of the hamadryad and krait, deadliest of snakes; home of giraffe-necked women and headhunters, of elephants and teak, of British tiffin and British rule and Buddhism, where the murder rate is three times that of the nearest competing country and where *dacoit** and *thuggee** vie with the ten types of malignant malaria to reduce the census figures.

Toungoo was Burma at its worst. The former British troop barracks which housed the A.V.G., huts made of

*Dacoit is the term for a robber belonging to an armed gang; a thuggee is a fanatical religious killer who employs the strangle hold for the greater honor and glory of the god Kali.

27

bamboo and teak, might have dated from the Sepoy Rebellion for all they offered in appearance and comfort. Here the weary A.V.G., stretched out on army cots after a blistering day, engaged in its first battle, the unending battle with the pests of Burma. Mosquitoes sang and swooped. The local rats bit the buttons off their clothes and squeaked defiance. Mildew coated walls, clothes, and furnishings. At meals, the boys employed knife and fork in gingerly duels with various eight-legged intruders. Sometimes they won, sometimes they yielded the plate to superior force and retreated to dream of mother's pies and cakes back home. Often they'd walk or bicycle along the dusty path to Toungoo and search the shops for anything edible in a tin marked "U.S.A." Some of them got sick, from malaria, dengue fever, and dysentery, and all of them cursed their fate and longed for their new base at Kunming to be completed.

Naturally morale suffered. A few kicked over the traces. Soon the word spread through Burma and into China that these volunteers were not angels at all, but brash young human beings who quarreled and complained and violated the tenets of Chesterfield. Observers forgot that "single men in barracks don't grow into plaster saints." Everyone was pretty skeptical on the question of how these turbulent strangers would perform under fire.

# CHAPTER FOUR

More Tomahawks were flown up from the CAMCO assembly yards at Rangoon, the A.V.G. suffered its first casualty, and school started in Toungoo.

John T. Sommers of Middletown, Ohio, former staff sergeant in the U.S. Army, was shot in the pants on the road to Mandalay, a victim of the boys' fondness for target practice with their side-arms. He was walking along the road with a companion where he heard a whirring sound and simultaneously felt an unpleasant sting. John thought that was too strong a blow for even a Burmese mosquito. He looked around, and yes, there was the guilty party, another A.V.G. boy who had been trying to shoot a crow.

Chennault took his pilots into the classroom, first, to brush them up on the schooling they had previously acquired in U.S. Army and Navy aviation. He then analyzed the Japanese aerial practice, calling to mind his years of observation to tell them just what Jap formations and individual pilots could be expected to do in any given situation. He said that their Tomahawks had four principal advantages over the Japanese planes: they were speedier on the straightaway and in the dive, and they were sturdier and better armored. The Japs could climb faster, turn more quickly and in general out-maneuver the Tomahawk in a dogfight. Therefore, the A.V.G. plan of attack must prevent the Jap from employing his superior features while forcing him into positions where his weaknesses could be attacked.

Chennault sternly warned them against individual heroics. Over and over again he reminded them that daredevils die early, that he had no use for daredevils. They could not avoid danger, of course. Danger was their business. But their duty to themselves and to their job was to minimize risk at every point while achieving a maximum of results.

"These Tomahawks of ours may be somewhat dated back in the States, now," he said once. "But out here, ten thousand miles away, their value is almost beyond computation. They cannot be replaced. Five million dollars couldn't get another one here today. Nor ten million. And don't forget your own value, to yourselves, your families and friends, to the Chinese you're fighting for, and to the Government that made you the highly trained specialists you are. You're irreplaceable, too. I don't know how to assess all this in dollars and cents, but boys, remember this: something a lot more precious than millions of dollars will ride with you on every flight."

He laid down two more commandments: they were never to waste precious ammunition that had also to be transported halfway across the world; when the target was there, within range, they were to give it all they had, then get away fast without waiting around for the post mortem.

Then, their commander sent them into the air, to teach them in action the teamwork, tactics, and gunnery approaches he had described on the blackboard. From five to eight hours a day he rehearsed them in the Bible according to Chennault. There was nothing revolutionary in his teaching, basically; no "Superman magic." It was the theory and practice of military aviation as Chennault and others had taught it to other American Army and Navy pilots back in the States; and now applied to the special problems presented by the planes and pilot training of the Japanese military system. Particularly he drilled them in the "blind spots" of the various Jap types, those sections of the planes from which no answering fire could come.

But schooldays were fatiguing business amid the odors and insects and filth and dripping heat of Toungoo. All of them grumbled at the routine of discomfort and work, and a few relieved their feelings by verbal pot-shots at Chennault. Said they: "Who is he to preach—this rather elderly adviser on military aviation to a country that has no military aviation?" All that the most dejected of them desired, of course, was something to fight besides the mosquitoes and boredom of Burma.

Their spirits were not lifted by the death of John D. Armstrong, of Hutchinson, Kansas, who was killed in a collision with Gil Bright. Gil bailed out successfully. This was the first death in the A.V.G. Maax Hammer of Cairo,

Illinois, and Peter F. Atkinson, of Martinsburg, West Virginia, also died as a result of accidents in training.

Soon after the start of the camp at Toungoo, the Japanese reconnaissance discovered this unusual activity, and thereafter the Kyedaw Airdrome received occasional visitors from the Jap base across the mountains seventy miles to the east. The Tomahawks on the ground were concealed in brush, surrounded by high earthworks to protect them against anything but a direct hit. The ground crew supervised native labor in the building of a "dummy" airdrome four miles away, as a further precaution. But until long after December seventh, the Japs never bombed or strafed Toungoo. Maybe they took photographs. Maybe they were afraid. Well, if they were, the ground crew decided, they'd make them more fearful. Eriksen E. Shilling, an Army flier from Washington, D.C., recalled some folklore to the effect that the Japs, an island people of fishing fleets and navies and odd religious beliefs, entertained a wholesale fear of sharks. So, with Chennault's approval, they painted the red mouth and flashing teeth and evil eye of the tiger shark on the noses of the P-40's. But other planes in other wars had used this same insignia. The A.V.G. wanted something different and distinctive, for in spite of their grousing and misery, they were slowly building up in themselves an *esprit de corps* that demanded expression.

Their leader had anticipated them in this. Chennault was already in communication with David Corcoran and Harry B. Price of China Defense Supplies, Inc., back in Washington, trying to evolve a distinguishing mark for his little aerial army. Chennault had suggested the figure of the falcon, swooping on its prey, and many artists had contributed their version of what form this emblem might take. None had quite hit the general fancy. Then Corcoran and Price invited the Walt Disney Studios in Hollywood to try an expert hand at the job, and from the brush of Henry Porter, a Disney artist, issued the figure of a Bengal tiger with two comically ineffectual wings, flying bravely through a "V" for "Victory." The tiger was as distinctive and charming a creation as Mickey Mouse or Grumpy. Chennault was delighted. The pilots of the American

Volunteer Group became "The Flying Tigers."

They christened their squadrons. The First became the "Adam and Eve" as that had been history's original pursuit, and the planes of this squadron blossomed with an action shot of Eve getting her man in the Garden of Eden. The Second Pursuit Squadron decided on the name and figure of the "Panda Bear"; the Third became "Hell's Angels," with a rather un-angelic female form painted below the cockpits of their ships. The selections were made only after lively discussion and argument. Most of the art work came from the hands of Shilling, Stan Regis, Bill McGarry of Los Angeles, and Allen (Bert) Christman, the only professional artist in the Group, who had originated a syndicated cartoon serial called "Scorchy" Smith for the Associated Press Feature Service. "Scorchy" was a daring aviator; so was his creator.

The world-shaking news of December 7, 1941, came over the radios of the A.V.G. and ended their ennui immediately. A few of the Navy fliers had seen service at Hickam Field near Pearl Harbor, and as the reports came in of American defeat and humiliation there, these fellows fairly ached for action. They took to loitering meaningfully around Chennault's headquarters, in the hope that their presence might inspire him to send them hunting Japs then and there.

Orders weren't long in coming. On December tenth, Arvid Olson of Chicago, squadron commander, was sent with his "Hell's Angels," twenty-five fliers and twenty-one Tomahawks to Mingaladon Airdrome outside Rangoon where a slim R.A.F. force was already established. On the same day the move from Kyedaw Airdrome—the welcome move—was begun, for now the main base at Kunming, China, awaited occupancy. Most of the ground personnel started off on the long journey over the Burma Road in trucks and Studebaker touring cars, leaving the pilots to fly the planes up later. The departing travelers shed no tears as they looked their last on Toungoo, that suburb of Gehenna.

During their training the A.V.G. had lost a dozen of the ninety Tomahawks actually delivered to them, and many of these were now grounded awaiting repairs and replacement parts. They had used up a considerable amount of ammunition in target practice. New planes, tires, and parts and large supplies of ammunition had been promised for November delivery, but failed to arrive. But a war was waging, the men had received what training time had allowed, and the American Volunteer Group was ready for action.

Ready for action? To tackle the mighty air power of Imperial Japan? Well, Chennault now had eighty pilots, backed by a ground force of one hundred and thirty-two mechanics and armorers. (There had been three deaths, and some resignations, illnesses, and firings.) For lack of spare equipment only fifty-five Tomahawks could take the air at the same time. Thus the full fighting strength of the A.V.G. in December 1941, on the brink of the great adventure: with outmoded pursuit planes; no bombs, no bombers; and not enough ammunition for five straight minutes of air fighting. Even Leonidas at Thermopylae had three hundred men, to protect a narrow pass. Chennault's tiny force had to guard a transportation system nearly fifteen hundred miles long against one of the strongest air forces in the world.

But the Tigers were ready, willing, and impatient.

# CHAPTER FIVE

The First and Second Squadrons took off in their planes from Toungoo for Kunming on the afternoon of December eighteenth, over the worst flying country they had ever seen, a country of jungle, mountain, swamp, and gorge. They had heard glad tidings of their new base at Kunming, the capital of the Chinese province of Yunnan and northern terminus of the Burma Road. Kunming, perched on the great plateau of Yunnan five thousand feet above sea level, was cool, it was new, and it was China. Awaiting them was a new airdrome and two good modern hostels, replete with shower baths, library, hospital service, tennis courts, and a baseball field, a pistol range, and Chinese cooks reputed to be expert in the technique of American ham and eggs.

But their first experience in Kunming was saddening. The Japs had been there before they arrived. Parts of this city of five hundred thousand souls were a smoking shambles. In the dusty litter of the streets they saw worse sights than ruined homes, worse sights even than the sorrow of the bereaved, the agony of the wounded, and the bodies of the still unburied dead. For it is the grisly fancy of exploding bombs to strike legs and hands and heads from human bodies, and these mementos of the bombing were visible in many places. Thus the Tigers had their introduction to the horror of war. The Chinese of Kunming went quietly and calmly about the task of restoring some sort of order to their blasted city. To them it was an old story, accepted and stored in bitter memory against the future. But to the men of the A.V.G. it was astounding and infuriating. Every last one of them was glad, then, that he had come to do something about such evils as this.

The next day was December 19. The First Squadron under Robert J. Sandell of San Antonio, Texas, was in the "ready" shack a half-hour before dawn, eager to revenge Kunming. If they had needed any spur to action, they had it now. But the Japs did not come back.

Sandell and five others of the "Adam and Eves" made a dawn patrol next day, the twentieth, but the Japs stayed away, while the morning dragged endlessly along. The Second was also on the alert, waiting. Nevertheless, something was going to happen, they knew. Something had to happen. They felt it in the air. They felt it in their bellies, where danger taps its warning with a red-hot needle. They pulled hard and deep on their cigarettes, waiting. In the parking area and along the edges of the field the Tomahawks with their shark-snouts seemed alert and fervid for action, too, as they received the ministrations of the ground crew. Then, just as the pilots feared they were to be robbed of their desire, the radio spluttered and spoke. The operator tore off his earphones and dashed into Chennault's office, with the pilots crowding in after him. The message read: "Ten Jap medium bombers are coming from the south; just sighted sixty miles away."

The General ordered Newkirk to go up at once and check the enemy position and in a minute "Scarsdale Jack" was off on his first business trip against the Japs, accompanied by Bert Christman, Don Bernsdorf of Minneapolis, and Gil Bright of Reading, Pennsylvania. The four Tigers sighted the ten bombers thirty miles to the south, and as they flashed this word back to the radio room, Chennault ordered them to return and protect the field, while Sandell and his "Adam and Eves" took over the battle. Sandell immediately went up with George Burgard of Sunbury, Pennsylvania, Charley Bond of Dallas, Enair Mickelson of Fergus Falls, Minnesota, Bob Neale of Seattle, Fritz Wolf of Shawano, Wisconsin, Bob Little, Ed Rector of Marshall, North Carolina, William Bartling of Middletown, Indiana, Jim Cross of Huntsville, Missouri, and five others for what was to prove the first and last time that the Tigers would ever outnumber the Japs in battle.

Newkirk and his three companions did not appear over the field promptly, as instructed. Everyone knew what they were up to, of course. They were having the first crack at the Jap anyway. But soon they came along, the others staying aloft while Newkirk came down and leaped from his cockpit black with anger. His guns had jammed on the very first burst, and he had no pleasant words for his armorer. As he took off again the sound of bombs exploding at a

35

distance were heard. That indicated good news. That meant the Japs were dropping them in the jungle; that the Japs were in trouble, and plenty of it.

The two-way radios in the Tomahawks didn't function during the battle, so the men in the "ready" shack had to wait for the defenders of Kunming to return. After some anxious minutes thirteen of the fourteen planes of Sandell's First Squadron appeared and the boys hurried out on the field to meet them.

It had been a "pipe." The Japs had never had a chance and seemed to realize it as soon as the First Squadron thundered down at them. Then it had simply been a matter of picking them off as they ran for home, diving, climbing and diving again until six of the bombers were crashing in flames. Four Japs escaped. The boys couldn't determine who was entitled to the credit for these victories, so they agreed to split the bonus money evenly among themselves. In the high excitement of their first combat they'd been too preoccupied for such bookkeeping details. And anyway, they were more interested in what had happened to Ed Rector, the missing Tiger.

After the victors filed a complete report of their action with Chennault, they checked the warning net for news of Ed. He had been seen limping away for an emergency landing, just after bringing down a Jap bomber with a blast from underneath. It was tough country, and when at nightfall they stopped their search near the impenetrable jungle below their recent battleground, they feared they had lost their friend and comrade.

But the next morning Ed telephoned headquarters from a near-by town to report himself alive and well. That started the day perfectly for the A.V.G., and when the First Squadron took the morning off to see the sights, they found themselves the worshiped heroes of Kunming. The grapevine had carried the news of their victory into every shop and home, and as they walked through the streets the Chinese greeted them with wide smiles and cheering calls. The kids of Kunming followed them in jubilant parades, the bolder among them yelling the words *"Fei Hu"* (the Chinese for "Flying Tiger") over and over again to direct the attention of their elders to the heroes. When a Tiger entered a shop he had an audience comprising every citizen who could wedge his way within the doors. Kunming was delighted with its defenders. After four years of enraged helplessness under the bombs of their enemies, they had at last seen the tables artistically and devastatingly turned. They were grateful, and they wouldn't let the Tigers forget it.

But the happiest man in Kunming was Claire Chennault. He sent a radiogram to his brother Joe in Washington, which read:

"We win first one, six pigeons to nothing."

From the hostel the boys telegraphed their pals at Mingaladon Airdrome in Rangoon to report the victory and gloat over the luckless Third Squadron, doomed to that hell-hole of inaction and boredom known as Burma. All the action was going to be around Kunming, they assured Olson. Olson and the Third disgustedly concurred in this viewpoint, and their savage words of disappointment rattled back over the wire to the high delight of the "Panda Bears" and the "Adam and Eves."

The Tigers could fight, but they couldn't read the future.

Word of the aerial victory over the Japanese spread quickly through the province of Yunnan, luring the people of the hills to the city to see these brave strangers from beyond the seas and their marvelous wagons that traveled through the sky. The visitors came by bullock-cart and sedan chair, on ponies and on foot, and the Tigers had a busy day. So did their interpreters, the Chinese youths from Christian colleges who had been assigned to serve the A.V.G. The Tigers would relate, first, the reasons why they were there fighting for China, then the interpreter would pass that information along to the visitors and give them a little time to consider it. Then, in a variety of dialects, questions about the airplane would flood the interpreters. They would try to explain what an airplane was, and what it did, to these simple people who had never seen a plane until that day. The visitors would listen and ponder what they heard, and wonder who was crazy—they, the interpreter, or the khaki-clad stranger who spoke in such a strange tongue. So at last the Tiger involved in this labyrinth of language and doubt would take the easy way out by climbing into his cockpit and settling the whole matter by demonstration.

37

Kunming looked good to the Tigers. No longer did they feel like strangers in a strange land. The climate was good, the hostel comfortable, and the Chinese cooks, one of whom had been chef for the U.S. Gunboat *Tutuilla,* actually functioned on such necessities of existence as liver and bacon, ham and eggs, chicken livers, pancakes, and American coffee.

Presiding over their hostel was Major General Huang Jen Lin, a prominent Chinese Christian leader with the title of director general of the War Areas Service Corps. General Huang was six feet three, weighed two hundred and fifty pounds, and sympathized completely with the boys' interest in good food and lots of it. For one American dollar a day, which also included lodging, he set forth the following:

| | |
|---|---|
| Breakfast: | Three eggs, bacon, hot cakes, butter, jam, marmalade, coffee. |
| Luncheon: | Soup, four vegetables, a meat course, dessert, and coffee. |
| Tea: | Cakes, sandwiches, and tea. |
| Dinner: | Soup, salad, four vegetables, meat, dessert, and beverage. |

And to crown this bargain he turned up with what was undoubtedly the rarest article in all of China—an ice-cream freezer. Ice cream—in ancient China. And beer, whisky, chewing gum, American magazines, and swing music records. Maybe this would prove a decent war after all.

The men of the A.V.G. now had sewn on the backs of their shirts and jackets their identification notices, which were decorated with the flag of China and bore the Chinese inscription:

"I am an aviator fighting for China against the Japanese. Please take me to the nearest communication agency."

This was intended to be the passport to the base, should they happen to be forced down somewhere in the wilds of Yunnan. The boys snickered at this label, but later on its

38

presence was to save the lives of a couple of them who had been driven to emergency landings in the jungle.

They were delighted also with their airdrome at Kunming, the product of the same tireless hands and spirits that had wrought the miracle of the Burma Road. And particularly impressive was the efficiency of the airplane detector system (the "warning net") which the Chinese had set up under the direction of Chennault in a vast circle surrounding their base. On the eastern and southern periphery of this were posted the "interceptors," Chinese volunteers with portable radio transmitters, some of them stationed within eyeshot of those Jap airdromes and emergency fields which reconnaissance had spotted in Indo-China. Within this circle was a second circle, one hundred miles away, and another only fifty miles distant, and strung along these lines were men with transmitters and expert knowledge of all types of Japanese aircraft. So whenever a Jap plane prepared to take off from any field within fifty minutes' flying distance from Kunming, the base knew almost immediately just what kind of ship it was and in what direction it was headed.

Deliverance from Toungoo, a few creature comforts, the victory over the Japs, and Kunming's admiration combined to make the Tigers at least livable to each other during those first days in Kunming. They bestowed the accolade of "The Old Man" on Chennault, and began to appreciate the hard job he had had with them and the efficiency of the organization he had built. But as the twenty-first and twenty-second went by without a flutter of activity, their tempers took on edge again. After all, they were here to fight a war, not to eat ice cream and view the sights. Their state of mind was accurately described by a young Chinese lad assigned by his teacher to act as an interpreter for the A.V.G., with the warning that he might encounter harsh language in his new post. After his first day at Kunming he wrote this note:

"My Kind Teacher: I am interpreter for Lieut. L—— He is with good heart and loud speaker. In first five minute conversation with me he remark 'Godamit' thrice. I understand your meanings."

# CHAPTER SIX

In Rangoon, where Olson and the "Hell's Angels" perspired and fretted, the people of the British and American colonies were pretty certain they were sitting on and under dynamite. They anticipated that the Jap onslaught on Britain's Asiatic dominions would not long overlook this principal seaport of Burma, the hub of its rich rice, petroleum, and lumber industries. They had reason to believe that the Burmese, eternally resentful of British rule, would embrace any invader who offered them something different, even if it were only a change in shackles. And they realized that the local military garrison was too pitifully inadequate to deal with a fair-sized native riot, much less a Jap invasion by land, sea, and air. Rangoon was a city with the jitters, ripe for panic.

Of course, by the very nature of the place, its polyglot population, and conflicting national interests, this city of five hundred thousand people could not have been expected to possess the fortitude of Chungking or London. It was not a truly Burmese city at all, but an unmelted mélange where the one hundred and twenty-five thousand Burmese were in minority to the one hundred and fifty thousand Hindus and the seventy thousand Muslims from India. The Indians provided most of the labor, the twenty thousand Chinese operated the shops and stores, and the thirty thousand Americans, British, Anglo-Indians (half-castes), and other foreigners ran the industries and dominated the town.

The presence of twenty-five American boys at Mingaladon Airdrome, where they shared facilities with the Royal Air Force, only emphasized to Rangoon the insecurity of its position. Everyone knew that the R.A.F. had only thirty-six antiquated Brewster-Buffalo pursuit ships and that the pilot personnel was small and inexperienced. Rangoon shook its head despairingly. Twenty-five kids from America, untried in battle; fifty or so from England, Australia, and New Zealand, also sprouting their first wings. What resistance could they offer to the mighty power which had already pulverized Pearl Harbor and Hickam Field, conquered the air over the Philippines, and was now sweeping triumphantly through the South Pacific?

All day long on the 22nd of December the rumors raced through the city. The Japs were reported in the Bay of Bengal with a huge battle force of carriers and warships. Their armies had been observed on the Thailand frontier a hundred thousand strong. To the fear-stricken native populace every one of Rangoon's million crows that took to the sky that day seemed almost certainly a Japanese bomber.

At Mingaladon Olson's Third Squadron was composed principally of former U.S. Army fliers. These included William Reed of Marion, Iowa; Robert Smith of Los Angeles; Tom Haywood of St. Paul; George B. McMillan, of Winter Park, Florida; Ralph N. Gunvordahl of Colorado Springs; Parker Dupouy of Seekonk, Massachusetts; Freddie Hodges of Memphis, Tennessee; Bob Hedman from Webster, South Dakota; Paul J. Greene of Glendale, California; Henry J. Gilbert, Jr. of Lovell, Wyoming; and Neil G. Martin of Texarkana. Among the others were Charles Older of Los Angeles, from the Navy, and two former Marine aviators, Ken Jernstedt of Yamhill, Oregon, and Ed Overend of San Diego.

Rangoon awoke with a start on December 23 to the terrifying whine of an air raid alarm. But nothing resulted except a tautening of every nerve in town. When the second call of the sirens also proved unnecessary, the people cursed the over-zealous civilian spotters and started on the day's work. At about eleven o'clock the sirens again sounded. They were ignored for a while, but when they continued their hair-raising turmoil people began to wonder. There were explosions and the bark of anti-aircraft fire; then with every Rangoon eye turned skyward, the Jap bombers appeared, eighteen strong, high over the river and coming for the docks.

At Mingaladon, the pilots had inadequate warning but a dozen Tigers and fifteen R.A.F. planes got into the air. At twenty thousand feet they beheld the oncoming second wave of the invaders, thirty bombers escorted by twenty pursuits. The battle was joined above the river, the Tigers

41

going directly for the bombers and leaving the R.A.F. to handle the Jap pursuits. Ken Jernstedt, "Hank" Gilbert, and two others tackled a formation of twenty-one bombers, Jernstedt giving one a squirt from the side and seeing it burst into flame as he dove past. Gilbert poured his fire into two others in his dive, but he was hit by a cannon shell from a turret gun and fell, the first Flying Tiger to be killed in combat.

Charles Older got his first bomber, which burst into a ball of flame and fell with ammunition and bombs exploding in mid-air. It is probable that the second death of a Tiger that day was caused by this accidental fusilade from Older's victim, for Neil G. Martin of Texarkana crashed in the wake of the bomber. Older sent another Jap crashing soon after, and Ed Overend of San Diego drew his first blood of the war.

Meanwhile some of the bombers had got through and dropped their bombs along the docks, whence columns of white smoke rose like geysers. Many of the Jap pursuits swept low over the streets, machine-gunning civilians and starting other fires. The Tigers confined themselves to holding the other bombers away from the wharves, and soon Robert Smith of Los Angeles had chalked up his first victory, a Nakajima bomber. Paul J. Greene, after pouring his burst into another, was swarmed on by two Jap pursuits, and had to bail out. The Japs went for him on the way down, one aiming for Paul and the other pouring bullets into the parachute. Paul was not hit but his 'chute was so perforated that he landed hard, injuring his spine.

The fight was furious but short-lived, as the Japs had seemingly not expected such resistance. Besides the deaths of Gilbert and Martin and the crack-up of their planes, Greene's and George McMillan's Tomahawks were demolished. The R.A.F. reported the loss of five planes with their pilots. The total haul of Japanese was figured at six bombers and four pursuits. The defenders had slightly outscored the Japs numerically. But having in mind their own high ratio of losses, they knew they would have to do much more than outpoint the invader in the future if they were to maintain any sort of aerial defense for Rangoon and the Road.

They had heard Chennault and Captain Aldworth and

other veterans tell them that "there's no substitute for being shot at" in the training of a combat pilot. They agreed, and they felt sure that the experience gained in that first battle would serve them well thereafter. Now, if only the British "warning net" would function in time so they could get "upstairs" before the Japs came over, and if only the promised ammunition supplies would arrive, and if only they could get something decent to eat, and a bath and some uninterrupted sleep—well, the "Hell's Angels" knew they would hold up their end of the war. They were "blooded" at last.

At Mingaladon after the battle, as the ground crew swarmed over the wounded Tomahawks, patching and repairing, the Tigers examined their ships. An armorer pointed out three tiny holes in the cockpit armor of Charley Older's plane, five of the same in McMillan's and four in Overend's. The toughened steel had meant the difference between life and death for those Tigers. Most of the Tomahawks had a dozen or more other bullet holes through the fuselages and in the tail assemblies. Yet these battered and perforated ships had survived the battle and come home to fight another day. The Tigers had been dubious about all that extra weight of armor and the general bulky construction of their Tomahawks. Their doubts were ended. Their ships could take blows as well as deliver them.

Rangoon had been devastatingly bombed. Fires raged in many parts of the city, and the streets near the docks, where the Japs had aimed their loads, were lost behind a wall of smoke. Three hundred dock workers had been killed in the one direct hit the Japs scored on a warehouse. A thousand other workers, fleeing up one narrow roadway through a poor tenement district, had been felled by a bomb exploding directly in their path. Their bodies lay as if cut down by a gigantic mower. In one square in a shopping district, Jap machine-gun fire had killed hundreds of women and children. On every hand were wounded and dying. Near the railway depot the Tigers saw a crowd gathered around a downed Jap bomber. They investigated this proof of their marksmanship, and were surprised to see that it carried a single fourteen cylinder motor patterned on an American Pratt and Whitney design.

43

Near by were the bodies of the crew, their clothes torn into shreds. An officer lay with his long curved *samurai* sword that seemed a curious weapon for a soldier of the skies.

The next morning, the twenty-fourth, they heard stories of bizarre and gruesome incidents, of looters who had robbed the unattended dead and sacked homes in the bombed sectors; of hospitals filled to overflowing with premature babies and their stricken mothers; of strange freaks wrought by the bombs, freaks too ghastly to think about or to relate. The A.V.G. had found little to admire in the British preparations for aerial invasion. But now, on the sad morning after, they saw the British volunteer service working with the smooth precision they had copied from their compatriots' experience with bombings in London. The fires had been subdued by volunteers working all through the night, and others had cleared most of the debris from the streets and were now busy filling up the bomb craters and pulling down the ruins of houses. All that day the body disposal squads tossed corpses into their trucks, and though the official casualty list announced a total of one thousand dead and one thousand injured, it was understood that more than three thousand people had been killed.

But the British made one mistake of omission—the kind of mistake that loses battles and wars. They had forgotten to provide for the maintenance of the Indian coolies on the job at the wharves and warehouses and in the important municipal services. One experience of the havoc and terror of a bombing had been enough for tens of thousands of these workers, who promptly packed their belongings and started for anywhere outside the city of Rangoon. Long lines of refugees already choked the roads leading to the north and west, many of them headed for their native India.

Business men appealed to the civil and military authorities for an extension of martial law that would have held these laborers to their tasks, but the responsible officials hesitated, for fear of an uprising, and the chance was lost. The normal activities of Rangoon, third greatest business center of Britain's empire in Asia, were almost completely paralyzed all through the twenty-fourth. Clerks, errand boys, servants, hospital orderlies, and street cleaners—the Indian and Burmese parts of the population—had joined the dock workers in flight.

Men with important jobs to get done went out into the country to harangue the refugees with promises of bonuses if they would return to work. A very few of them did go back, in the late afternoon, after learning that no Jap planes had appeared over the city throughout the day. The Anglo-Indian employees stayed faithfully at their posts in the telephone and telegraph system, but on that eve of Christmas the other public services were at a standstill. Worst of all, not a drop of gasoline or a pound of freight was moved from the docks.

It was a day of grief and suffering and fear and hunger for Rangoon. And it was a sad time for the A.V.G., who mourned the loss of "Hank" Gilbert* of Lovell, Wyoming, and Neil Martin of Texarkana, in the Rangoon fight, and of Lieut. Lacey Mangleburg of Athens, Georgia, on a ferry trip.*

*On receiving the news of his son's death, Henry Gilbert, Sr., enlisted in the Navy to "carry on" for his boy. And "Hank's" mother wrote to the United China Relief, 1790 Broadway, New York City, enclosing $100 for "the suffering Chinese people whom our beloved son had come to know and love."

**On December 23 Eric Shilling of Washington, D.C., Lacey Mangleburg of Athens, Georgia, and Ken Merritt of Arlington, Texas, were assigned to ferry three new Curtiss Wright Type 21 interceptor pursuit ships to Kunming. They flew to Lashio, refueled, and set off northward. But the fuel was faulty, their engines failed, and they were forced to try emergency landings in rugged mountain country. Lacey Mangleburg, a former U.S. Army lieutenant, was killed in the crash of his plane. Merritt and Shilling narrowly escaped death when they pancaked their own ships into the mountain.

# CHAPTER SEVEN

> *"God rest ye, merry gentlemen!*
> *Let nothing you dismay."*

Dawn of Christmas Day, 1941, saw the Tigers on the alert at Mingaladon, eager for a crack at the Jap after what they conceived to be their failure on the twenty-third. They had spent the night reviewing that battle and their mistakes of tactic and judgment. They agreed that they had underestimated the agility of the Jap pursuits, which in a chase could turn inside of them and gain the advantage in a twinkling; they must, therefore, extend their power dives considerably in distance, using their superior speed to elude the Jap fighters and then circling and climbing at top speed until they regained the "drop" on their foe. Facing superior numbers, as they undoubtedly would, they must aim their dives at the thickest concentrations of the enemy, with the hope of knocking out two or more of them in each eight-mile-a-minute downward dash. And they resolved to devote their major attention, when conditions permitted, to the Jap bombers, who constituted the prize prey because of their greater value, their large crews, and the fact that their deadly cargoes held the really serious menace to Rangoon.

It had been a little like the old pre-game powwow of their basketball and football days back home. But here in the red dawn of Burma the stakes were not field goals and touchdowns, but life and death.

They went out on the apron to watch the sun rise, one of them recalling Rudyard Kipling's twisted geography which had it coming "up like thunder outer China 'crost the Bay." The sun rose, as usual, and despite Kipling, over the dripping jungle to the east.

One of the ground crew came from the radio room with the information that Radio Tokyo was on the air, claiming overwhelming victories near Manila and gloating over the destruction of American aerial resistance throughout the Philippines. A little later the Tokyo announcer sardonically reminded Rangoon that it could expect a bundle of Christmas presents shortly.

An hour dragged on. Two hours. They waited, as the sun's mounting heat picked up the dew in preparation for Burma's daily steam bath. They thought of home, home on Christmas morning. They were homesick, and admitted it. Christmas dinner? They speculated on what they would have had in the States. They knew too well what they would have in Burma. Perhaps a can of corned beef. Perhaps nothing at all. Perhaps—? They didn't say it, but they knew it might well be a mouthful of blood and dust.

As nine o'clock came and went without an alarm, Olson, expressing lack of confidence in the British warning system, sent three of the Tigers aloft for reconnaissance. At nine thirty one of them, George McMillan, flashed the word that a huge Jap bomber force was on the way sixty miles out. In the same minute the British sounded the alarm. Olson dispatched three Tigers to reinforce McMillan and his flight, and another formation of seven to follow immediately. The boys ran for their ships, shouting encouragement to each other, welcoming the relief of action.

Ten miles from the field the Tigers confronted an awesome exhibition of Japanese military power, sixty bombers escorted by twenty fighters. As they came over the Rangoon River, the Japs separated into two approximately equal formations, one heading for the town and the other for Mingaladon Airdrome. The Tigers, conferring quickly over their two-way radios, decided to take on the Japs aiming for the docks. Shouting their battle cries, they swooped on the enemy, delivering full blasts into the leading bombers, then showing their tails to the Jap fighters before the latter could get within firing range. McMillan and his flight were busy far above, picking off a Jap fighter here and there and leaving the bombers to the main A.V.G. force below. Tom Haywood, Charley Older, and "Duke" Hedman blasted a bomber apiece in the first attack, and shattered the classic Jap formation. Which was just what the Tigers wanted. With the bombers stringing out in pairs and trios, the Tigers raced "upstairs," fought off the Jap pursuits, assumed their positions for the dive, and screamed down for the kill. It was a kill. In a moment five of the big

Jap ships were falling like winged ducks, while others were dropping their bombs in the rice fields and scurrying toward the east.

Then as the Tigers began a furious pursuit, out of a cloudbank to the east appeared a fresh wave of Jap bombers, twenty of them topped by eight fighters, a clean-up squad dispatched to put the finishing touches to the Christmas Day devastation of Rangoon.

The Tigers promptly abandoned the chase of the vanquished to deal with these newcomers. The proximity of the Jap wave left no time to soar for altitude, so the Tigers resorted to the "uppercut," going low and then in a wide line coming up under the Jap bombers with all guns blazing. Los Angeles' Robert Smith's first victim exploded at such proximity that parts of cylinders from the Nakajima bomber's motor were imbedded in his Tomahawk. On this soaring attack, Ed Overend's plane was hit by a hundred bullets and limped out of the battle, seemingly headed for a crash.

"Duke" Hedman, a stocky farm boy from South Dakota, got three bombers and a fighter. He sent the first one eastward with a burst at three hundred yards, then carried on past and hit a second when only fifty yards away. As he came steaming back for altitude again three Jap bombers left the formation. "Duke" gave them his personal escort service until they were well away from their fighters, then he picked off one, which exploded in mid-air. Returning to the main scramble he knocked out a fighter after a ten mile chase, then rushed for Mingaladon and landed with one pint of gas left in his tanks.

By this time the R.A.F boys were fighting off the force of Japs that had started for the docks, and sent several spinning into the river below. So well did the British resist here that of fifty ships tied up along the wharves, only one was struck by a bomb.

Further out, the Tigers were paying all their attention to the bombers, too, and the Jap fighters evidently had no instruction or inspiration as to how to proceed against such unorthodox procedure. So they remained above the main battle. Now and then one of them would leave formation to escort a wounded bomber as it deserted the fight and started for the Jap base to the east. With the mass of the invaders soon panicked into so many waifs and strays by the fury of the Tigers' attack, Paul Greene, Parker Dupouy and George McMillan took after the retreating ships to bestow the *coup de grâce.*

Dupouy was set upon by two Jap pursuits, and finding his guns jammed after dispatching the first, deliberately collided with his remaining assailant. The fragile Jap plane fell apart, but Parker, with four feet of his right wing sheared off, "babied" his stout Tomahawk back to Mingaladon safely.

Other narrow escapes that day were experienced by General Sir Archibald P. Wavell, Britain's Commander for India and Burma, and Gen. George H. Brett, Commander-in-Chief of the U.S. Army Air Forces in Asia, who landed on Mingaladon from Chungking in a CNAC (China National Aviation Corp.) transport just as Jap bombers were reported approaching. As the big plane came down one of the Tigers dashed out to meet it in a truck, gathered up the two commanders and took them to shelter. When the Japs didn't appear at once, Wavell and Brett insisted on going to headquarters. They started up the field, when suddenly hell broke loose from a huge squadron of bombers directly above. The generals saw the rest of that raid from a friendly ditch near by.

Watchers on the streets of Rangoon saw the great battle of the sky change quickly into an utter rout of the invaders. In all directions but toward Rangoon, the Japs with whole skins were racing away from those horrible shark snouts that spouted death, leaving their stricken companions easy prey to the Tigers. Into the paddies and the surrounding jungle below fell burning Jap planes, shredded planes, the splinters of planes demolished by the explosion of their own fuel tanks, and planes simply shot out of control. Jernstedt, Older, McMillan, Hedman, Bill Reed, and the others were knocking them down right and left and center, from above and from below, in the most annihilating defeat ever suffered by an air force in the Second World War.

When it was all over, eleven of the thirteen Tomahawks that had gone aloft went back to Mingaladon Airdrome, fuel and ammunition almost spent, fuselages and tails dotted with holes, but with the day's work well done. They were received vociferously by the ground crew, armorers, and administration people of their own force and by the R.A.F., joined by scores of American and British who had witnessed their triumph and hurried out to give their praise and gratitude to the defenders of Rangoon.

Mingaladon, the Tigers learned, had had its share of the battle. Fifteen R.A.F. planes had engaged the thirty Jap bombers who originally pointed for the airdrome, and eight of these had been brought down and chased off before a single bomb had hit the 'drome. One Jap bomber had attempted a suicide crash on the headquarters building, missed it narrowly and now lay in smoking ruins in an adjoining field, the bodies of its officers and men lying like so many rag dolls where they had been thrown clear of the shattered ship. The R.A.F. had lost five of its men with their Brewster-Buffalo fighters. The Tigers? Well, where were Ed Overend of San Diego, and George McMillan, their only missing combatants? They didn't have to wait long for news of Ed. He supplied it himself, arriving at the field in a Model T Ford, driven by a grinning Indian lad who had found him walking along a road on the outskirts of town.

Ed reported:

"I had just knocked a wing loose on a bomber and was after him trying to knock off the other when I heard something like hard rainfall hitting my ship. I knew that was a Jap on my tail, so I tried to pull away from him. But the controls had been shot into a jam. All I could do was go forward in a flat dive. So I hunched down and gave it all I had. When I got to around five thousand feet, I saw I was well away from the fight with nothing to do but save my own hide, if I could. The fuel was practically gone so I couldn't try for Mingaladon. Down below there seemed to be nothing but hills and the puddles around the rice fields. I thought of taking to my parachute, but I knew darn well we couldn't afford to lose that Tomahawk of mine. So I retracted my landing gear and eased her down, ever so gently, plump into a shallow swamp. It was a rough landing, but safe. Then as I started to crawl out, what should I see but a gang of natives coming for me with knives and sickles, yelling bloody murder. But when they saw I wasn't a Jap they all smiled—and baby, so did I."

McMillan showed up next day, riding in state in a bullock cart, with one ankle bunged up but otherwise unharmed. He had worked his way painfully through the jungle during the night and found his native taxi driver early in the morning.

After the battle, stories gushed from all the Tigers, with the groundlings flocked about them marveling at what these youngsters had done that day against the vastly superior numbers of the experienced Japanese air force. It was too soon to approximate an account of the slaughter, but as they talked, reports came by telephone and person of the wreckage of Jap planes all up and down the countryside. British Military Intelligence already had a corps of searchers accumulating the evidence, having been charged with this responsibility by CAMCO, which was empowered to pay the $500 bonuses to the Tigers only on conclusive proof of Jap planes destroyed.

Final accounts of the victories varied widely. Officially credited to the A.V.G. were thirteen Jap bombers and ten fighters, a total of twenty-three planes. Leland Stowe, the American war correspondent who flew to Rangoon immediately after news of the astounding Jap defeat reached the outside world, reported that the Tigers had brought down at least twenty-eight planes. The Tigers estimated six additional victories over the Gulf of Martaban, where the Japs had sunk with the evidence. In any case, it was established beyond doubt that of the one hundred and eight Japanese planes participating in the two Christmas Day raids, the Tigers with R.A.F. help, had knocked out at least thirty-six, or thirty-three per cent. In addition, the Japs had lost not less than ninety-two pilots and bomber crewmen, as compared with only five deaths for the R.A.F. and none for the A.V.G.

The individual records of the Tigers that day showed four Jap planes brought down by Charles Older of Los Angeles and four more dropped by "Duke" Hedman. Rarely, if ever before, had a military aviator destroyed so many enemy ships in one day.

Other A.V.G. victories were listed as follows: three Japs

51

to Bob Smith of Los Angeles; and two each for Parker Dupouy, Ed Overend, Ken Jernstedt and Bill Reed. From Kunming Chennault telephoned his congratulations, and notified the men of the Third Pursuit Squadron that they could look forward to a few days' leave shortly.

But the most welcome message of all came over Radio Tokyo that Christmas night, when the victors were taking their ease. An unpleasant voice stated: "We warn the American aviators at Rangoon that they must cease their unorthodox tactics immediately, or they will be treated as guerrillas and shown no mercy whatsoever." The boys rolled on the floor when they heard that one. They stayed on the floor, rolling, when Radio Tokyo, sensing its duty to the national morale and simultaneously forgetting its previous dire warning to the Tigers, reported blithely that thirty Anglo-American planes had been downed over Rangoon and that the city was now without air protection.

But despite their disastrous defeat, the Japs had gained a most important objective. This became apparent on the morning after, which found the city in complete paralysis of its customary functions. The streets were deserted, post and telegraph offices, markets, filling stations, and ships closed for lack of operating personnel. It was evident that the little people of Rangoon were having no more of the Jap bombs, even in view of the victorious defense on Christmas Day and the fact that damage wrought by a few bombers that reached the city had been paltry indeed. Only one wharf in the entire three miles of dock space had been hit. Not a warehouse had been touched. Nevertheless, all day long on the twenty-sixth not a worker appeared to move a pound of lend-lease supplies toward the Burma Road and China. In the evening CAMCO, by offering two rupees* a day to coolies, double the usual pay, lured a crew back to work from a camp ten miles out of town. There were, of course, plenty of whites and Anglo-Indians remaining in the city, but the coolie—the backbone of all Oriental countries—simply went A.W.O.L. Those who had not started for India settled down in refugee camps and some of these were gradually returned to service on the understanding

*A rupee was worth 32.5 cents.

that they would be furnished free transportation into the country at night.

The Japs stayed away on the twenty-sixth and twenty-seventh of December, possibly to count their wounds and certainly to devise a new strategy for dealing with the terrible shark-faced killers of Burma. The Tigers fretted at this enforced inactivity, especially because they now had a good supply of tracer bullets, which had turned up in the cargo of a Catalina flying boat which landed at Rangoon on Christmas Day, on its way to Australia. The pilot of this ship had seen some of the fighting, and he figured that if the Tigers could do any better work against the Japs with tracer bullets that he had just witnessed, they were the boys to have them.

On the twenty-eighth, the Japs inaugurated their new plan. The Tigers had plenty of warning and ten of them went up to engage the enemy, who appeared in the surprisingly small force of ten bombers and five fighters. The Japs, however, refused battle, and the encounter developed into a game of aerial tag with the Tigers having to chase their prey all over southern Burma. After almost two hours of this, in which the Tigers had downed only two Japs, the remaining thirteen raced for home and the Tigers returned to Mingaladon to refuel and discuss this puzzling development. They were enlightened immediately by a new alarm reporting a strong Jap force of thirty on the way, ten bombers and twenty pursuits. Only four Tomahawks could immediately take the air (the others were being refueled or under repair) but a dozen of the R.A.F. joined the Tiger quartet and met the Jap force forty miles to the southeast. The twenty Jap pursuits immediately engaged the fourteen defenders, while the bombers ignored the battle and steered straight for Mingaladon.

The intent was clear—to catch the remaining Tomahawks and Buffaloes on the ground and bomb them to perdition while the defense was busy elsewhere. But before the bombers could reach the airdrome, six other Tigers had raced aloft and from 20,000 feet dove into the thickest of the Jap formation. Within five minutes eight of the Jap bombers had crashed in flames. Two of them got through and dropped their loads on the edge of the air-

53

drome where the pathetically weak anti-aircraft* fire was not effective above three thousand feet. The batteries did succeed in knocking out a Jap fighter who came low over the field for a strafing attack.

With the principal enemy force dispersed, the Tigers and R.A.F. men went off to join their fellows who had taken on the first Jap wave. It developed, however, that the sole duty of this force had been to draw the main strength of the A.V.G. and the R.A.F. well away from Mingaladon so the Jap bombers might carry out their assignment in comparative peace.

*For two days after this first action of the "ack-ack" batteries, the British civil authorities combed the city for "the Fifth Columnists who had sent up flares to guide the enemy to the airdrome": a sparkling example of the co-ordination existent between British military and civil departments in Rangoon.

# CHAPTER EIGHT

The "Hell's Angels," dirty, hungry, but covered with glory, departed on the morning of December twenty-ninth for Kunming, grumbling at being withdrawn from the war they had begun so brilliantly. Newkirk and his squadron wished them peace and poor hunting, and stood by at Mingaladon for the Japs.

Newkirk's Second Squadron, the "Panda Bears," was composed largely of former U.S. Navy pilots. Among them were David "Tex" Hill of Hunt, Texas, son of a Texas Ranger chaplain; Tom Cole of Clayton, Missouri; Henry Geselbracht of Glendale, California; Noel Bacon of Randalia, Iowa; Robert Lahyer of Otis, Colorado; Ed Rector of Marshall, North Carolina; Frank Lawlor of Winston-Salem, North Carolina; Johnny Petach of Perth Amboy, New Jersey; John "Gil" Bright of Reading, Pennsylvania, a former Princeton pole vaulter; and Lynn Hurst of Beaumont, Texas.

The city they had now to defend was two hundred thousand people short of its normal population. Over fifty thousand Hindus and Muslims had begun the long jungle trek toward India. Other thousands were on the roads northward to interior Burma. But most of the evacuées were huddled in huge camps along the roads and in the fields from ten to twenty miles outside Rangoon. Forage provided their only food supply. In desperation some of the men came into the city on the twenty-ninth seeking work, but fear held most of them in the country where hunger and disease now began their deadly work.

Shortly after noon the air raid alarm sounded, and Mingaladon heard that thirty bombers and fifteen Jap pursuits were on the way. Newkirk took a dozen Tigers with him, and the R.A.F. sent ten Brewster-Buffaloes. They sat in the sun twenty-two thousand feet up and fifeeen miles out waiting and trying to understand the messages that came from Mingaladon over their two-way radios. But they could make nothing of the garbled sounds emitted by these inefficient mechanisms. After they had been up an hour without a look at a Jap, suddenly out of a bank of cloud to the eastward came a great attacking force of about forty bombers and twenty pursuits. When the Japs sighted the Tigers and the R.A.F., the big formation split up into two divisions, one heading for the airdrome and the other coming straight for the defenders of Rangoon.

Newkirk flashed the warning back to the field (the radios worked well from sky to earth) then ordered the Tigers to the attack, as the British moved to intercept the formation aiming for Mingaladon.

The Tigers, most of whom were facing their first battle, thundered down on the Jap fighters from above and went on through the formation of bombers, giving them a full blast of fire right at the start in the hope of fracturing their formation. As the Tigers pulled out of their dives and raced "upstairs" again, they saw four Jap bombers and two fighters fall out of the battle enveloped in flames. But before they could regain altitude the other Jap fighters came at them in dives, while the surviving bombers swept on toward the city. Newkirk sent six of the Tigers to intercept the bombers, and then led his remaining five out of the path of the decending fighters. As the Japs roared downward the Tigers narrowly escaped their bursts, then turned and followed them down to ten thousand feet, picking them off one by one. Newkirk got two in quick succession, the first of his string; Frank Lawlor got three, and one each was chalked up by "Tex" Hill, Bob Layher, and John Gil Bright. The rest of the Jap fighters ran for home, and the Tigers turned back to fight off the bombardment of Rangoon which was already in progress.

A huge column of smoke indicated the Japs had already hit the railroad station. Far out toward Mingaladon, there were other fires. The Tigers, racing for the city proper, hoped that their fellows at the field had been able to get into the air before the Japs arrived.

The bombers over Rangoon were now without any fighter protection, and were having all they could handle from the first Tiger attack. With other defenders coming for them now, the bombardiers quickly unloaded their racks and ran down low to prevent the Tigers from diving on their backs. But the Tomahawks could hop the hedges too, and in this chase out of Rangoon, Tom Cole, Ed Rector, Noel Bacon, and Fred Hodges got their first "certains." With the Jap turret gunners working furiously, the pursuers were hit by hundreds of bullets. Bert Christman had to bail out, finally, and the other Tigers, running low on fuel and bullets, went back to see whether they had an airdrome left to land on.

They almost didn't. The other Jap formation had bombed Mingaladon from end to end; the R.A.F. buildings were in flames, and fires rose from several planes and trucks that had been caught along the British end of the field. Headquarters building was on fire, and several shacks that housed the tools and equipment of the A.V.G. ground crew were already smoking ruins.

The field itself was a patchwork of bomb craters, but even as the Tigers circled to land, they saw the ground crew fill in the last of these along the runway and signal them to come down.

They had not lost a man in the battle, Bert Christman turning up almost at once as sound as ever. The R.A.F. had lost six planes with their pilots, and reported five Jap bombers and two fighters shot down. The Tigers accounted for eighteen victims, compared with their loss of one Tomahawk. The Japs once more had learned that it was expensive to attack the city of Rangoon.

The thrilling experience of first combat is described in the diary of one Tiger:

"Suddenly we had an alarm. The leader called out, 'Scramble!' And we dashed out to our planes and ran up to 20,000 ft. I timed it. We did it in less than 20 minutes. I thought it was just another false alarm. Suddenly out of a cloud appeared ten Japanese I-97 fighters. The four of us dove on them. I charged my guns and turned the switch. I was breathing hard and fast. We went down almost vertical, but they dodged us, and my bullets went behind the one I aimed at. The others had told me how fast the little devils could get around on our tails, so I barreled straight down. I must have had my throttle wide open in my excitement, because when I started pulling out and looked around to see if anyone was on my tail, I nearly blacked out. I eased back on the throttle, leveled out and climbed sharply. I spotted the Japs again and started after one who seemed to be flying straight and level. As he turned sharply and dived I missed miserably. I kept on going down and as I climbed I felt a little more at ease and took my time.

"I could see none of our P-40's. The Japs were there in a swarm. I dived, shooting a long burst into a twisting, rolling fighter and I am sure I damaged his machine. He dove out, but I ignored him because I was looking everywhere for fear of a Jap on my tail. I climbed again and started after another one. He went into a cloud. I thought I had lost him, but then I figured that if I waited he would come out again. He did, right in front of me, within 200 yards. I gave him all six guns and I could see my tracers hitting the target. I soon was right on him and had to lift my right wing to miss his left one. As I did I saw his cockpit burst into flames. I laughed hysterically and yelled out loud: 'I got one! That pays you back, you devils!'

"I guess I was acting like a maniac, but it was a great thrill as I saw him fall in smoke. I wheeled sharply, patting my 50's like a farmer caressing his favorite horse, and looked for more. I saw four heading for home and as I neared them they separated and started circling. As I dove on the most isolated one he attempted an Immelman turn. I caught him with a full blast of my left wing 30's. (My 50's were jammed and so were my two right 30's.) A thin trail of smoke left his tail as he ran into the clouds. I couldn't find him there but I am almost certain he was a goner.

"I was crazy for battle now and I went after the other three. As I climbed I kept messing with my 50's and finally got one to work. As I came close to the three Japs the leader waggled his wings and turned gently to the left. His right wing man fell back from the V and fell out. Their strategy was obvious. I knew that if I went for the leader the wide wing man would close in on my tail. I feinted toward the leader, then wheeled sharply in a flipper turn at the wide wing man. He dove out and my bullets went wide. Suddenly it came to me that I had been fighting for almost an hour and my gas was low. I ran back to the field, gave the observation tower a buzz, did a 'victory' slow roll and landed.

"As I taxied back I noticed a crowd surrounding a plane on the edge of the field. It was a Jap fighter. The pilot had tried the old Jap trick of getting something even if he had to die himself. He had missed a Blenheim bomber by a few feet and crashed near by in a thousand pieces. As I walked up an R.A.F. man picked up the Jap's helmet, with part of the pilot's head and throat hanging out. The poor devil had been decapitated. The R.A.F. boy grinned and pointed thumbs up. But I couldn't grin, looking at his other hand and what it held. After all you have to give them credit.

"Tonight in spite of everything I am a very tired but contented person. At last I have done something."

The rest of the day and night the boys' only worry was where and how to obtain food. The bombardment had driven most of the remaining workers into the country, and the food supply system was dormant. The larders of the British and American homes, where most of the A.V.G. were billeted, finally yielded a scanty delicatessen of sardines, jam, and crackers, but that was all. The A.V.G. and nearly everyone else in Rangoon went hungry to bed that night, while the city government enlisted volunteers to patrol the city against looters and to work in the food warehouses and stores.

The Japs continued the war that night via Radio Tokyo. The broadcaster began with the customary paean of praise to the Japanese Air Force and the usual announcement that the American Volunteer Group had been wiped out all over again. Then he promised Rangoon that ten thousand Jap paratroops would descend over the city the next day to complete formal annexation.

Neither paratroops nor bombers appeared, however, so the Tigers spent their time foraging. The order of the day was to find a chicken, trail it to its lair, where there might be eggs and other chickens. The famished Tigers followed this order to the letter.

On December thirty-first the Japs repeated their attack plan followed on December twenty-eighth, with a force of twenty planes coming over promptly at ten a.m. They kept twelve Tigers busy chasing them for two hours, then left hurriedly, having accomplished their mission of wearing down the defenders. For just as the Tigers landed after this sortie, a big battle force of sixty planes was reported on the way.

Eight Tomahawks joined nine of the British in the air at once, and they caught the Japs ten miles out. Again the Jap fighters swarmed all over their foes with reckless courage, releasing the bombers who headed straight for Mingaladon. That was the sole objective now. Rangoon would be forgotten, evidently, until that hornet's nest at Mingaladon had been destroyed with its last plane and its last pilot.

When the bombers were free of the fight, the Jap pursuits fled a few miles toward the east then circled and came back to their assignment of protecting the bombers. The Tigers didn't catch up with them until they were over Rangoon, and then watchers in the streets below got their first full view of the fangs and claws in action. The Japs fought with suicidal fury. Undoubtedly their instructions were to do or die. When a plane was stricken, the Jap pilot did not bail out, but came winging toward earth and death strafing the street below. The Tigers pounded them hard, and so fragile were the Jap pursuits that some of them splintered in the air under a burst from the .50 and .30 caliber bullets of the Tomahawks. Ten Jap planes had fallen on the city before the other fighters gave up the struggle. Then the Tigers took after the bombers who had just left Mingaladon with a few of the "Panda Bears" in pursuit. Their combined force raked the Jap retreat with murderous fire for thirty miles, bringing down five more bombers.

At Mingaladon they threaded their way to earth amid the huge hole dug by the bombs, and helped to fight the fires that beset several of their buildings. The 'drome had taken another fearful pasting. One maimed bomber pilot had deliberately crashed with his full load near the headquarters building, destroying several British trucks and damaging two Tomahawks. Several members of the ground crew had been injured, none seriously.

Individual victories recorded that day were attributed to Frank Lawlor, Ed Rector, John E. Petach, Fred Hodges, "Tex" Hill, Newkirk, Reed, and Henry Geselbracht.

The newspapers of Rangoon by this time had two standard headlines: the "banner" gave the day's box score of the Flying Tigers and the R.A.F.; the lesser dealt with news from the hunger and refugee fronts. The A.V.G. monopolized not only the newspaper space but also the social spotlight, and thereby brutally offended the more decorous British who insisted on dressing for dinner whether or not there was any dinner to eat.

After dark those men of the A.V.G. who were not on duty flooded the expensive Silver Grill cabaret, arrayed in their simple khaki shirts and trousers, sporting their side-arms, with their "mosquito" boots bearing the stains of the day's work. This was bad enough. But when the Americans appeared with handsome and happy Anglo-Indian girls who had never dared approach these exclusive precincts before, and proceeded to teach the girls the joys of jitterbugging, Rangoon society was shaken to its foundations. It had its own Mason and Dixon Line. Proud nostrils were distended almost to the breaking point. Complaints were filed with the management. But the management had no desire to start another war, so the Americans and their girls went on gamboling, and gradually the starched élite of Rangoon steeled itself to the phenomenal spectacle of people actually having a good time. It was unheard of in Rangoon, but in wartime strange things happen.

The orchestra at the Silver Grill, by request, soon began the practice of playing "The Star-Spangled Banner" as well as "God Save the King" at the end of each night's dancing. Some of the local British had never heard the American anthem, and in their ignorance remained seated during the opening bars of its first rendition. These innocent offenders were speedily waited upon by delegations of the A.V.G. Thereafter, international etiquette was scrupulously observed there and in all other night spots of Rangoon.

The Silver Grill had plenty of Scotch whisky, gin, and beer, but its kitchen had suffered with every other in the city. The place now served only one course, at a buffet, and the patron took what was there or went hungry. Invariably, there was cauliflower. Sometimes, there was practically nothing but cauliflower, ineffectually festooned with a lone sardine or a driblet of cheese. Why cauliflower should have triumphed over bombings and business stagnation remained an eternal mystery. But as a memento of Rangoon, the American Volunteer Group will hate cauliflower to the last breath of its last survivor.

Despite the cauliflower, the Tigers celebrated New

Year's Eve in true American style, with a little confetti, and much skylarking. So much, in fact, that four Tigers failed to show up to fight the war next morning. They were fined $100 apiece by Squadron Commander Jack Newkirk. The fines were later remitted.

# CHAPTER NINE

As 1942 began, the American Volunteer Group was world famous. War correspondents of the leading American and British newspapers and press services were established in Rangoon, pounding out the rich "copy" which the Tigers supplied almost hourly.

This was the grand old story of David versus Goliath, in modern dress. Here they were, a few American boys, novices in war and in life as well, delivering the only victories the whole Allied cause could boast over the Japanese military system whose power and skill and guile in warfare were now fully appreciated everywhere on earth. Day after day these American kids, half-starved for food, short on ammunition, were taking their patched and bullet-riddled fighting planes into the sky to beat back armada after armada of the war-wise Japanese air force. The odds they surmounted in each battle were unprecedented. No wonder the world marveled.

How did they do it? What were they up against?

For a groundling to acquire some comprehension of this most dangerous business—the business of the combat pilot, he should observe a modern fighting plane in action on the target range at night. In repose the ship in the darkness will seem tiny and fragile. Let the motor open up to its full power, though, and in the deafening roar the plane will suddenly assume the sinister aspect of a strange wild beast. Then let it strike with its fusilade of tracer bullets flying for the target. Imagine yourself four miles up and on the receiving end of all that concentrated murder, not from one enemy but from five or eight to ten, and you may understand a little of what the Tigers faced over Asia.

Their Curtiss P-40 Tomahawk was a sturdy, well-armored pursuit plane, faster on the straightaway than the Jap fighter, and possessing more firepower with its two .50 caliber and four .30 caliber machine guns. The early Jap pursuit type in Burma, the Nakajima fighter, carried only two machine guns. It disintegrated easily under a burst from the Tomahawk, and the pilots were without armor-plate protection.

The Japs had built for maneuverability, and achieved it. Against them, the Tomahawks were so slow in climb and turn that the Tigers were forbidden ever to challenge a single Jap in dogfight.

The Jap Nakajima bomber, the usual Burma marauder, had American-designed twin motors that drove it faster than the Jap fighter on the straight run. It carried a crew of five, and threw considerable lead from its 37 millimeter cannon in the turret, and a remote control gun in the tail, which was operated from the pilot's seat. The Tigers quickly learned to dodge the sweep of that tail gun and attack the bomber from above, outside the arc of the turret gunfire.

An often fatal weakness of Jap ships was their lack of bullet-proof fuel tanks. Many of them blew up in midair. That never happened to the Tomahawks.

The Jap airmen had all the fatalistic and fanatical combativeness of their race. The A.V.G. called it "guts." The Japs had been trained for their job during four years of operations over China. They knew their business.

The Tigers were learning their business the hard way, but they were learning it well. By January first, they had brought down some sixty "certains," plus a total of one hundred and twenty Jap pilots, bombardiers, and other crewmen. The Tigers had lost only two pilots and three planes in combat. The paddy fields and jungles around Rangoon were dotted with shattered pieces of Japanese airplanes. Across the bay to the east, where searchers could not go, other wrecks of Jap planes were sighted from the air. How many had already limped from the Rangoon battles to crash further on in Thailand will never be known. What was known, in Tokyo and everywhere else, was that a few American kids were knocking the "face" and the daylights out of the Imperial Japanese Army Air Force.

The men who best appreciated the exploits of the A.V.G. were those Americans and Chinese responsible for moving the goods from the docks toward China. They saw the victories not only in terms of courage and glory, but in actual military objectives achieved. After December twenty-seventh, until the evacuation, the Japs were never able to drop a bomb on the wharves and warehouses which held many millions of dollars' worth of irreplaceable supplies and matériel. They could never knock out the railroad northward to Lashio, either. So China got these essentials for its armies, simply because the Tigers protected them from above while the skeleton crews of coolies under their American and Chinese bosses worked the clock around.

The men of the A.V.G. formed many good friendships in Rangoon among the R.A.F. personnel, with the Anglo-Indian journalists who hymned their praises daily, and with the representatives of the various companies dealing in lend-lease administration and aid-to-China generally. These concerns included the South West Transportation Company, which handled all shipping from Rangoon to China; the Universal Trading Corporation, originally formed to represent the Import-Export Bank and later directing Chinese exports to the United States; the Yunnan-Burma Railway Company, which employed many U.S. Army engineers and other technicians in charge of construction of a railway intended to supplement the Burma Road; and China Defense Supplies, Inc., administering all lend-lease business. Then there were the CAMCO crowd, the pilots of the Chinese National Airways Corporation, the celebrated line which operated planes on a strictly "bad-weather" schedule to avoid Japanese attacks; the American oil and motor car company representatives, free lance business adventurers and war profiteers, and various newspaper men and magazine writers.

Many of the Americans had come from Haiphong, in Indo-China, and called themselves "The Transiteers." They were seasoned to the tropics, to somnolent officialdom, red tape, "squeeze," and bombs, having engaged in war business to China until forced out of Haiphong by the Japs. They had a song of their own, which the A.V.G. helped them sing in every cabaret and on every possible occasion. To the tune of "Madelon," one of its few polite verses ran:

"When your *entrepôt fictif** is going strong,

*Bonded warehouse.

65

And your trucks and your cargoes all go wrong,
What do you do, to forget Haiphong?
Baie d'Along, Baie d'Along, Baie d'Along!"*

Two other organizations devoted to beverages and group singing were the "Burma Roadsters" and the "Short Snorters," into which A.V.G. men were enthusiastically received. The qualifications for membership in the "Roadsters" were two in number: to have traveled the Burma Road, and to own a ten dollar Chinese banknote. On this a member must have inscribed the signatures of all other members, and failure to produce the bill on demand cost a penalty of one dollar American. The "Short Snorters" was restricted at first to air-line pilots, and used an American dollar bill for membership card.

These men played hard, but most of them worked harder marshaling the panicky coolies amid air raid alarms to perform the necessary work of the port.

On January first the defense of Rangoon was reinforced by five pilots and five planes of the First A.V.G. Squadron.

The newcomers were greeted by the whiskered and famished boys of the Second Squadron with a volley of questions, all dealing with food. After a stage wait they insured their welcome by producing five fat turkeys and a bundle of other viands, the gift of a Chinese general. No turkeys ever won more applause or suffered quicker demolition. The boys expressed a little of their appreciation by a collection among themselves which raised 5200 rupees ($1700 American) for the Chinese war orphans cared for by Madame Chiang Kai-shek.

The A.V.G. dined in peace. No Japs came over on the first of January, or the second, which gave the ground crew needed opportunity to "doctor" the battered Tomahawks. The Tigers had already learned to marvel at the wonders their mechanics could work on their torn and perforated half-wrecks.

On January second, the A.V.G. learned that Chinese ground forces had crossed the frontier into Burma and were awaiting orders to reinforce the British Empire armies under General Archibald P. Wavell as commander-in-

*Baie d'Along was an amusement center near Haiphong.

chief in India and Burma. The war was getting closer. Reports came in all day of Jap troop movements along the Thailand border. Rangoon, faced with this news and the accounts of uninterrupted Jap conquests in the Philippines and Malaya, added to its worries the new menace of a land invasion.

Early on the third, Newkirk, Bacon and "Tex" Hill delivered the first A.V.G. strafing of the important Jap air base at Tak in Thailand. Arriving over the field, they saw the Jap planes lined up in perfect formation, and immediately went down within a few hundred feet to blast the obliging Japs. Suddenly seven enemy pursuits, which they hadn't seen, swooped down on them, one getting on Newkirk's tail. Bacon tried to force this fellow off, whereupon another Jap let loose at Bacon from behind. Hill raced after this one, and the six planes roared low over the field scarcely ninety feet apart.

Newkirk sank his bullets into the long row of planes below, unaware of the mad pursuit behind him. A company of Jap soldiers dashed out onto the field, assumed solid formation, and began firing rifles and machine guns at the Tigers. Bacon forced the Jap fighter off Newkirk's tail with a burst that sent him into a fatal landing, the plane nosing over and breaking into flames. Hill shot down Bacon's assailant and another Jap, then headed for home with a leaking gas tank and out of ammunition. As Newkirk and Bacon passed over the soldiers, they gave them full bursts, killing a dozen or so. But the Japs maintained formation and kept shooting until the Tigers were out of range. Looking back, they saw seven Jap planes on fire.

At Mingaladon, after they landed, Hill congratulated Newkirk on escaping the Jap who had followed him over the Tak airdrome. Jack vehemently denied that he had been in any such danger until Hill took him to his Tomahawk and pointed out twenty-two bullet holes in the tail.

Before the strafers returned to Rangoon six more Tigers had gone up to intercept twenty-seven Jap planes. They were all fighters, and full of fight. The Tigers got two in their first attack, but five of the Japs "ganged up" on Bert Christman with a furious crossfire that smashed an aileron and tore his rudder to pieces. Bert immediately took to his parachute, whereupon the Japs, forgetting *Bushido*,* tried to kill him as he descended. George Paxton of Abilene, Texas, moved to break up this shocking attack on a helpless airman, which violated the code of sky fighters in all armies except the Japanese. Paxton succeeded, at the cost of five bullet wounds in the arms and legs, but he managed to escort Bert safely to earth before leaving the battle. The other Tigers, observing this, attacked so furiously that the Japs again fractured the rules of *Bushido* by running away from a fight.

*Bushido*: the much-publicized Japanese code of martial chivalry.

# CHAPTER TEN

Generals Wavell and Brett had come to Rangoon on Christmas Day from Chungking, after discussions of strategy for the defense of Burma with Generalissimo Chiang Kai-shek. Two major problems confronted the commanders: whether Britain should pour all her military strength from India into Burma, or maintain her Indian garrisons at virtually full strength against possible Jap air and sea-borne attacks on India itself; and whether China should throw her armies into the defense of Burma or mount a strong offensive in Indo-China.

The Japanese, late in December, sought to keep Chiang's armies occupied in China by launching a powerful attack on the city of Changsha, where they had already been repulsed in three previous attempts. Here on January fifth the Chinese scored the first great land victory for the United Nations by annihilating the Japanese, who left fifty-six thousand, eight hundred and fifty-four dead on the battlefields.

But in January, except for Changsha, and the heroic defenses of Rangoon and Bataan, the Jap timetable for conquest of Asia and the Pacific was being triumphantly followed. Elsewhere in the Philippines and in the Malayan jungles the Japanese beat down resistance with alarming ease. Chiang insisted that Burma must be held, and offered Wavell all the battle-tested manpower of China that he might need for the job.

The importance of Burma to the Allied Nations was obvious: it was the link between China and India; it held the source of China's lifeline of supply; it not only adjoined Jap bases in Indo-China and Thailand, but could also serve as the springboard for an offensive across the entire line of Jap expansion in the South Pacific.

Chiang knew that Burma was poorly defended by a few battalions of raw, uncertain, native levies, trained and equipped for the parade ground, perhaps, but not for modern war. Wavell could bring in scarcely two divisions of Empire troops, British, Australians, and New Zealanders, and his entire aerial strength rested with the tiny forces of the A.V.G. and the R.A.F.

Early in January the Japs made their first night air raid, a tentative experimental sort of visit to test the caliber of Rangoon's defenses after dark. They found no defense, except the anti-aircraft fire of a few British ships in the river, and the "flaming onions" that were effective only up to three thousand feet.

Both the R.A.F. and the A.V.G. were now using "satellites"; the "satellites" were named "Johnny Walker," "John Haig" and "Zed," landing fields, twenty to thirty miles away from Mingaladon, as hiding places for their ships, and the Japs seemed to be searching for signs of activity on these fields as well as on Mingaladon.

After the first few unchallenged night raids, the Japs' feeling of security was so extreme that they came at around five thousand feet, with riding lights glowing. They would cruise for a while, searching for a target in the blackout below. Soon a series of blood-red flashes would light up the horizon, revealing the sinister shapes of the marauders overhead. Seconds later would come the rumble of the blasts, rattling all the doors and windows in the city. The Japs followed the phases of the moon meticulously, the first wave of bombers arriving over Rangoon exactly forty minutes later each night. The Tigers longed for a crack at the invader, certain that with this foreknowledge of their schedule, it would prove relatively simple to give them a sound beating.

But their Tomahawks lacked detector equipment for night fighting, and the boys decided against any more forays into the night blackness after the tragedy of January eighth, when Pete Wright, coming down after dark, was blinded by hydraulic fluid spouting from his damaged landing gear, and crashed into an automobile in which Ken Merritt of Arlington, Texas, was catching a few winks of sleep. Ken was dead when they found him in the wreckage.

January eighth also saw the loss of popular Charley Mott, whose plane took fire, apparently from anti-aircraft shelling, over Meshot airdrome on a strafing trip with "Tex" Hill and Bartelt. The three Tigers raked the field with machine-gun fire, destroying seven Jap planes on the ground, but after gaining altitude Mott's plane burst into flames and he "hit the silk." Hill and Bartelt left for home hurriedly when a force of Jap pursuits took after them, but they felt sure that Charley had landed safely. Radio Shanghai, a few days later, announced that Charley Mott was a prisoner of war, and then introduced a speaker purporting to be Charley himself. The speaker professed his newfound love for the Jap and his eternal hatred of the A.V.G. The boys at Rangoon said that neither "the words nor the music" sounded like Charley.

The night bombing continued with increasing boldness, fresh waves coming over at midnight, and again at 3 a.m. This made sleep pretty nearly impossible, but the men of the A.V.G. were not complaining, because at last they were eating regularly and well. A semblance of order had been restored to the food supply system, once the Flying Tigers had spread their protective wings over the city and the docks. There were thick steaks and chops and strawberries and cream at the Strand Hotel again. The walls of the Silver Grill echoed to the stamp of the jitterbugs and the massed voices of the Burma Roadsters and the Short Snorters. Many of the men were now billeted in the homes of American and British residents, who possessed sound cellars and generous larders. The crews of American ships arriving in Rangoon proudly played host to the A.V.G. on shipboard, where the boys luxuriated among steaks and chicken and ham and foamy beer while they swapped yarns of the war on sea and land and in the air. No longer did they eye the crows of Rangoon with gustatory speculation. No longer did the once-accursed Toungoo and its water buffalo meat seem demi-Paradise. An army flies as well as fights on its stomach, and the A.V.G. stomachs now carried this very necessary equipment.

A second "section" of the A.V.G. had been in the Pacific bound for Rangoon on December seventh. With the Japs in abrupt control of the sea these men and the planes accompanying them had been re-routed to Australia for service with the United States Army. Still, it seemed incredible that the two great English-speaking powers, the richest nations on earth, would leave the A.V.G. and the R.A.F. in Burma very long without considerable reinforcements.

71

Already several ships loaded with lend-lease supplies had been warned away from Rangoon by radio reports of the aerial invasion there, and had gone on to unload their cargoes at Calcutta. China simply could not be thus starved of supply, Rangoon assured itself. Under no consideration would the United Nations take a chance on the loss of Burma, the gateway to India, the keystone of Britain's whole imperial system in the East.

Rangoon joined the A.V.G. in the laugh that greeted a special broadcast from the Jap-controlled Radio Shanghai, which announced that the American Volunteer Group with its "thousands of planes" constituted the most important enemy Japan faced in Asia. The broadcaster assured his listeners that the A.V.G. would shortly be blasted out of the sky completely; and then, with weird Nipponese inconsistency, Radio Shanghai blared forth with "The Stars and Stripes Forever." The sign-off tune of the Shanghai station was invariably "My bonnie lies over the ocean." Could "bonnie" have been Mr. Kurusu?

Radio was a versatile weapon in this war. The Tigers had developed their own language for communication on their two-way sets as they flew into battle. If a Jap force of forty planes were sighted, the signal would be: "Forty pirates (or bandits) at twenty angels." That meant forty Jap planes at twenty thousand feet. Should the invader force number twenty bombers and twenty fighters, they were described as "twenty big rats and twenty little rats." When a Tiger had a Jap right where he wanted him, he'd yell wild imprecations as he delivered the finishing burst. The order to return to the field was always "Free Beer!"

The Japanese used a similar wave length to that of the A.V.G., and now and then as the Tigers were conferring via the ether a strange voice speaking English with the unmistakable accent of Nippon would cut in to call them dirty names. They welcomed these interruptions. Their answers would be swift, to the point, unprintable, and accompanied by immediate action in the direction of the heckler. The mortality rate among linguistic Jap pilots became very high.

On January ninth "Scarsdale" Jack Newkirk led four of the A.V.G. and six of the R.A.F. on an afternoon visit to the Jap airdrome at Tak in Thailand. With Jack were Noel

Bacon, Pete Wright, "Tex" Hill, and Percy Bartelt.

As the shadows lengthened over Mingaladon and the raiders did not return, the ground officers joined the crewmen out on the apron to search the sky. The radio elicited no news of the missing men. The sky was empty. In Burma the tropic night descends like a vast blanket, without any interval of dusk. They were fearful of what might have happened, when suddenly out of the east came the welcome thunder of many motors. As the first Tiger came along, almost scraping the tree-tops, he indulged in the "Victory Roll," which the A.V.G. had borrowed from the R.A.F. as a sign of good news. Then they came in and down, singly, with anxious eyes counting them.

"Seven! Eight! Nine! Where's the other two? Oh, there's one! And yep, there's the last one. Hotcha!"

As the victors taxied up to the apron, the watchers, British and American, flocked around to greet them with a flood of questions and a medley of accents, from Yorkshire and Texas, Lancashire and Missouri, Cockney and Yankee, Anzac and Chinese.

"We dived from ten thousand feet and caught 'em flat-footed, working on their planes," reported Jack Newkirk. "We blasted three planes and three trucks to smithereens on the very first run. Then we went back and really got going."

"We did that," said a Yorkshire lad of the R.A.F. "You should have seen Jack catch a supply truck. He drove the driver so crazy he ran wild into a burning plane."

Pete Wright chimed in: "Yah, but Jack, you're a lousy billiard player. Why didn't you carom that truck into one of the planes that wasn't on fire?"

The complete results of the Tak raid showed twenty-four Jap planes and three trucks destroyed in flames on the ground and the administration building machine gunned by a thousand bullets. The Japs hadn't presented a glimmer of defense.

Jim Howard of St. Louis* narrowly escaped death or capture the next morning on a return trip over the Tak airdrome with Newkirk and Hill. As they came over the

---

*Howard was born in China, the son of Dr Harvey Howard, of Peiping Union Medical College. Jim spoke Chinese fluently.

field, Jack, in the lead, saw two Jap fighters circling to land. He got both of them, then, as the Tigers strafed the field, Howard's guns continued to fire after he had turned off the switch. This caused such an immediate drain on the electrical system that his motor started to miss. By this time other Jap pursuits were chasing the Tigers. With bullets thudding into his ship, Jim let down his gear for an emergency landing, when the motor suddenly caught again. He soared clear of the trees skirting the airdrome with a Jap right on his tail. But Tex Hill came down, disposed of the Jap with a short burst, and the Tigers made good their escape. They reported five planes left in flames on the field, and three downed in combat.

With these repeated raids on Thailand air bases the Tigers were throwing the first offensive the Japs had encountered from the Allied Nations in the entire Far Eastern War. It was dangerous business to jeopardize their few planes and pilots in the strafing expeditions, where rifles and machine-gun bullets might strike a vital spot at any moment. But the Tigers' task was to protect Rangoon and the Road, and each Jap plane destroyed on the ground was one more threat removed from the war. But they constantly marveled at the air strength Japan had distributed through Thailand. When the first swift Navy "Zeros" appeared in increasing number, the A.V.G. guessed that the Japs were bringing up reinforcements from Malaya, where their control of the air was almost undisputed.

The British were promising reinforcements at Rangoon, too, and finally eight Westland-Lysanders observation ships arrived. The A.V.G. turned up its collective nose at these moribund crates, which could not attain a two-hundred-mile an hour speed if chased by a hurricane. But when the brave kids of the R.A.F. sailed off with the decrepit Lysanders to bomb Jap airdromes, the Tigers and their Tomahawks went along to protect them. The boys had no respect for the British military system in Burma, but they appreciated the quiet courage of the boys of the R.A.F. When some Chinese government officials flew down with four cases of Scotch whisky, a few kegs of beer and crates of bananas and oranges, the party was on the A.V.G. and the Britons were the guest of honor.

On January thirteenth Bob Sandell, commander of the

First of "Adam and Eve" Squadron, arrived in Rangoon to reinforce the Second. With Sandell came Charley Bond of Dallas, Bill McGarry and Dick Rossi of Los Angeles, Frank Schiel of Prescott, Arizona, and Greg Boyington of Spokane. Bob Neale of Seattle, vice squadron leader of the First, came down soon after with George Burgard of Sunbury, Pennsylvania, Jim Cross of Huntsville, Missouri, Bill Bartling of Middletown, Indiana, Robert H. "Snuffy" Smith of Eagle River, Wisconsin, Bob Little of Seattle, Louis Hoffman of San Diego, and John Croft of Trenton, New Jersey.

Most of these boys had not yet flown in combat. They came late to the Rangoon front, but they were destined to achieve some of the most brilliant victories recorded by the American Volunteer Group.

On January seventeenth Rangoon learned that the "Hell's Angels" had got back in the war near Kunming, with Charley Older, Tom Haywood, and George McMillan knocking down one Jap bomber apiece in the first foray the Japs had attempted there since the first battle on December eighteenth.

The day's work of January twentieth, as reported in the A.V.G. *News,* follows:

Tuesday, January 20, 1942.

WEATHER: Clear, sunshine, cumulus clouds, fairly warm.

RADIOGRAM received from Newkirk, Second Pursuit Squadron, Mingaladon, Burma.

"HOWARD AND HASTEY RECONNAISSANCE TAVOY NOTHING SEEN SELF AND MOSS AND NEALE AND BARTLING AND CHRISTMAN AND GESEL ESCORTED 6 BLENHEIM TO BOMB MESHOT STOP ATTACKED BY 7 ENEMY ARMY 97 FIGHTERS STOP BOMBERS PROTECTED OBJECTIVE DESTROYED STOP SELF DESTROYED 2 DEFINITELY PLUS 1 PROBABLE STOP NEALE SHOT DOWN 1 PROBABLE STOP MOSS MISSING LAST SEEN IN DOG FIGHT STOP CHRISTMAN 25

HOLES IN PLANE LANDED WITH PUNCTURE TIRE PLANE AND PILOT OKAY STOP FIGHT ON BURMA SIDE OF BORDER 3 MILES FROM OBJECTIVE STOP 19 OKAY 8 REPAIR TOTAL 27 STOP TWO BUFFALOES SHOT DOWN MOULMEIN TRYING TAKE OFF STOP COMBAT REPORTS AND CONFIRMATIONS BY SAFE HAND WHEN RAF GIVES THEM OUT END NEWKIRK".

Intelligence Report: The strength of Japanese troops in Tonkin now not only does not decrease, but even increases when compared with that in December last. It seems that Japan is fanning the war between Yunnan and the boundary of Yunnan, Annam, and Burma. Japan has instigated the Annamese troops to be responsible for the defense of the line along the Hanoi-Laokai Railway.

REPORTS of Activities of the Second Pursuit Squadron. Mingaladon, Burma:

Six (6) P-40s escorted 6 Blenheims on bombing mission at Meshot, Thailand. Took off at 1115. The P-40S flew over the Blenheims at 10,000' heading N.E. in direction of Meshot. 6 Enemy fighters were picked up at about 8,000' about 3 miles S.W.Meshot. Two more enemy aircraft appeared. The P-40s engaged them. Enemy aircraft flew in scattered pairs and their attack was initiated from above rear. One enemy plane coming down and the other one remaining overhead. Bombers bombed the Meshot aerodrome. Result of fight: 4 Probably enemy aircraft destroyed. One AVG ship destroyed. The pilot of this ship, Wing man R. C. Moss reports: "My engine burst into flames when two enemy ships jumped on me after I had shot down one enemy plane. I bailed out from 1,500' at about 7 miles on our side. I travelled for 14 1/2 hours by bullock cart, 4 miles by boat, and 14 miles by car which brought me to Moulmein where I caught a bomber home."

At 1705 a reconnaissance flight of 6 P-40s took-off for

Meshot aerodrome, Thailand. No enemy aircraft was encountered. The pilots observed a large fire two miles west of Meshot in Burma. It was noted that the runways at Meshot are distinctly outlined by white markers which may indicate that it is used for night work. The flight returned to satellite field at 1849.

The A.V.G. *News* was published daily by Mrs. Olga Greenlaw, wife of Harvey K. Greenlaw, second in command of the Group as its executive officer. Greenlaw had been a contemporary of Chennault in the U.S. Army Air Corps, and directed all A.V.G. operations in the absence of "The Old Man."

# CHAPTER ELEVEN

The naval victory of the American and Dutch fleets in the Macassar Straits cheered the Tigers at Rangoon, busy with their daily strafing raids of the Mesarieng, Meshot and other Jap airdromes in Thailand. In one of these Bob "Little Moose" Moss of Athens, Georgia, bailed out and was given up for lost. A few days later Bob drove up to the R.A.F. field at Moulmein in a handsome bullock-cart, after a long and perilous trek through the jungle. The British flew him over to Rangoon and a hearty A.V.G. welcome.

It was about time for a gigantic daytime display by the Jap bombing force, and it came on the twenty-third. Newkirk, Bert Christman, Frank Lawlor, "Tex" Hill and Fred Hodges of the Second Squadron encountered the first Jap wave over the Gulf of Martaban, ran through the "umbrellas" of a dozen fighters and hit the ten bombers below. Frank Lawlor got three of these in three successive dives, the others got one apiece. Christman's plane had difficulty in climbing for the fourth attack, and he was set upon by two Jap pursuits. Apparently badly hit, Bert flipped his Tomahawk over and entrusted his life, for the third time in a month, to his parachute. The other Tigers were busy with the remaining Jap force and did not see what happened.

When the second wave of Japs came over in the afternoon, fifty strong, the Tigers and the R.A.F. were ready for them east of Rangoon. The "Adam and Eves" entered this battle, Johnny Petach getting three bombers. That night twenty-one more rising suns were painted on the fuselages of the Tomahawks. These were the Tigers' "notches" for their victims. Among those who proudly watched the paint applied were Bill Bartling, Ed Rector, Noel Bacon, Bud Layher and Gil Bright of the Second Squadron; and of the "Adam and Eves," Louis Hoffman, Bob Sandell, Bob Neale and Robert "Snuffy" Smith of Eagle River, Wisconsin.

Bartling, on his second trip into the fray after refueling,

had ended up in a rice paddy with his Tomahawk full of holes. Noel Bacon got a bomber and a fighter before his plane was shot out of commission, but he landed the Tomahawk safely.

The next day Bert Christman's body was found in the rice fields. His parachute had been torn to tatters by many bullets, and Bert himself had unquestionably been the target for a machine-gunning fighter pilot during his descent. This pleasant, quiet lad, a professional artist and cartoonist, had spent much of his leisure time painting pictures of native life. They buried him that afternoon with full military honors. Rector, Hill, Petach, Bacon, and Geselbracht were the pall bearers. The boys resolved unanimously that the Imperial Japanese Army Air Force would be paid back in full for the wanton killing of Bert Christman.

It proved a bad week for the A.V.G. On the twenty-sixth Louis Hoffman, nicknamed "Cokey," the oldest pilot in the Group, was shot dead in his plane while defending against a bombing raid on Rangoon. Louis had been a member of the famous VF-2 fighting squadron of the carrier U.S.S. *Lexington.* At the age of forty-three he had satisfied the organizers of the Group that he was capable of competing with much younger men in the difficult business of air fighting. He left a wife and two children in Oceanside, California.

There was cheering news from Kunming on the twenty-fourth, which indicated that Olson, Older, Reed and their pals of the "Hell's Angels" were still in the war. On that day most of the Third Squadron escorted several old Russian bombers manned by Chinese pilots and crewmen on the first offensive foray conducted beyond the borders of China since the early days of the Manchu dynasty. The goal was the important Jap airdrome at Hanoi in Indo-China. There the Chinese dropped one hundred bombs on the field and the surrounding hangars, while the Tigers strafed Jap troop concentrations nearby. The visit came as a complete surprise to the Japanese, who failed to bring down a single attacking plane.

The boys at Rangoon detected the hand of "The Old Man" in that raid. For years Chennault had waited for the day when he could give the enemy a taste of the murderous medicine they had fed the defenseless Chinese. He had been using every appeal and every artifice he could think of to acquire some modern bombers; not merely for retaliatiory action, but to strike Japan in its heart at Tokyo. But there were no modern bombers in the entire world for China just then. So Chennault had employed the lumbering old Russian crates to support his point that the way to beat Japan was to attack it at home. The Jap reaction to the Hanoi raid bore out Chennault's argument. Radio Shanghai and Radio Tokyo screamed dire threats of vengeance, while the puppet French in Indo-China followed orders by protesting vehemently to Chungking.

In the Rangoon fighting of January twenty-seventh Gil Bright of Reading, Pennsylvania, and Raymond Hastey of Chipley, Georgia, took on seven Jap pursuits. Hastey was bearing down on one Jap's tail when he took a cross-fire fusillade from another, which knocked off his rudder and elevator. The Tomahawk zig-zagged crazily for a few seconds. the Jap firing and Hastey working furiously at the controls. As the Jap came in for the kill, the wounded Tomahawk suddenly swooped, and turned upside-down. That was enough for Hastey, who slipped his safety belt and dropped out head first. As he reported later:

"It was the first time I'd ever hit the silk. But as I fell the picture of Bert Christman with his 'chute full of holes was with me, and I didn't pull the cord. What speed I was making! I'd traveled maybe nine miles a minute once in a dive, but that was nothing to this. They say a falling body picks up speed as it falls. Baby! I was certainly some falling body.

"Well, the devil of it was I couldn't get my feet below my head. The only place I could look was up, and there was my ship coming for me with that shark's face grinning in the wildest spin you ever saw. There wasn't a damned thing I could do but let her come, so I let her, and she whizzed by as if I was standing still. But I wasn't. I was going so fast that I was sure no Jap could catch me."

In the next few seconds Raymond Hastey experienced, almost simultaneously, the deepest fear and the happiest sight of his life. As he plunged earthward, he heard a motor, and one groggy eye caught the outline of an oncoming plane. This was the finale, he told himself. But no, it wasn't a Jap. It was Gil Bright, escorting him, making sure that it wouldn't be a Jap. With that, Bob yanked the ripcord, and floated the rest of the way in style.

"I was throwing kisses to Gil all the way down," he said. "I saw my Tomahawk still spinning below me, and watched her as she cracked up. Pretty soon I was close to my destination, so I looked straight down, and there was a dirty looking pond waiting to receive me. I just missed it. So here I am."

Early on the morning of the thirtieth, Jap troop concentrations were reported near Moulmein, one hundred and twenty miles eastward near the Thailand frontier. The British asked the A.V.G. to send a strafing force against them. The Tigers were under no obligation to endanger their lives and their planes in this sort of action. Their Tomahawks were without armor-plate protection against ground fire, and a forced landing in that morass of jungle and swamp meant almost certain death. But Jim Howard, Ed Rector, and Tom Cole welcomed the assignment, and went off into an overcast sky. Tom, from Clayton, Missouri, was a Navy flier who loved combat and was constantly complaining because no Japs would ever come near him.

"Here I've been almost a month," he had said that morning. "All you guys get plenty of action, but when I go up all the little Nipponese ——s have urgent business somewhere else. One lonely Jap! That's all I've got to show for the whole darned war."

Below them near Moulmein the three Tigers saw a Jap infantry division moving along a narrow roadway through a forest. Rector stayed above as protection against possible Jap planes, while Tom Cole and Jim Howard went down to strafe. Tom took for his target a line of supply trucks, and dove perilously low. For some reason—it may have been that he was hit by shots from the ground—Tom didn't pull out of his dive, and his Tomahawk crashed into high trees and burst into flames. Howard and Rector returned to the base, to confirm the nearness of the Jap land invasion and to report the death of their comrade.

The first Jap land forces to invade Burma had crossed the Thailand border on January fourteenth, where they encountered the Burma Rifles near Tavoy. The Rifles retreated after a few salvos, in complete disorder, unmindful of the orders of their officers to hold a line. These officers were Britons, territorial volunteers from colonial business firms, and they knew nothing of jungle warfare. But with the gameness of their race the British marshaled some sort of defense against the invaders, who halted their advance, and waited. While the Japs idled near Tavoy, other ground troops filtered through the jungle and spread along the eastern, the Tenasserin coast, of the Gulf of Martaban. Wherever they met resistance they employed their new tactic of the false alarm, by which a few concealed soldiers would set off great numbers of firecrackers, and draw all the attention of the defenders, while the main force silently gained the objective. Here in the brush, as in Malaya, the Japs painted their faces green and traveled usually in parties of three, two men bearing machine guns and the other loaded down with ammunition. They wore rubber shoes, they kept going on a handful of rice a day, and were otherwise completely unorthodox, and completely successful. The Burmese Rifles could present no suitable riposte to such originality. The Japs fell silently upon their sentries from the trees, riddled them at their mess, grenaded them as they slept, and soon were in control of the full four hundred miles of the Tenasserin coast.

On January thirty-first the real invasion of Burma began with numerous attempts by the Japs to cross the Salween River. The British landed one crack division of Indian troops at Rangoon on February first, and rushed them to the west bank of the Salween, where they held stanchly. A Chinese division was encamped in the northern Shan States of Burma, more were over the border waiting for the call, and at Chungking the Generalissimo prepared to fly southward to investigate the defenses of Burma and India.

On February fourth a CNAC transport landed on the Kunming airdrome and two passengers alighted. One was a slightly-built Chinese, of middle age, who stood very erect in his plain khaki uniform. His companion was a slender, handsome Chinese woman. The man walked into the headquarters office, while the woman stayed behind to talk to the American pilot of the transport plane.

Ed Liebolt and Enair Mickelson of the "Hell's Angels" Squadron came out of the A.V.G. "ready" shack and noticed the lovely Chinese woman.

"Suppose she'd like to have tea with us?" said Ed.

"Why not?" replied "Mick." "Probably needs it after that trip."

They climbed into their open car as the woman left the plane and walked toward the A.V.G. shack.

"Of course she needs some tea," said Ed. "And anyway, she's cute. So here goes."

Ed started up the car, and stopped it directly in the woman's path. He tipped his hat, grinned, and extended the invitation. The woman smiled, thanked him in perfect English, whereupon "Mick" leaped out and helped her into the front seat. Then "Mick" climbed in alongside and they were off for the hostel. It might have happened in any American town. It has.

"I really think I should tell my husband where I'm going," the woman said.

"Never mind him," advised Ed. "He may be tied up for hours."

"Sure thing," said "Mick." "The service is terrible here. But say, tell us: where did you learn to talk such good American?"

The lady smiled. "Oh, I went to school in America. A long time ago."

Ed demurred. "A long time ago! Why, you're just a kid. What you doing down in these God-forsaken parts, anyway?"

She smiled again. "Oh, just traveling."

"Know who we are?" asked Ed.

"Oh, surely. Aren't you a pair of these American fliers I've heard so much about?"

They assured her that they were. They assured her that she was the grandest sight they'd seen in China. They assured her that she was in for a great treat at their hostel, and they reassured her about her husband.

"He may be delayed here for days," said Ed. "Can't get any service around this dump unless you're covered with

83

gold braid. What does this husband of yours do, anyway?"

"Oh, he travels," the woman said.

The boys arrived at the hostel and escorted her into their prized precincts with ceremony.

"The joint is yours," Ed told her.

The Tigers received their first shock as they entered the door. When the Chinese servants beheld the guest, their jaws dropped and they dashed away like men possessed, slamming doors madly behind them.

"Hey, what is this?" yelled Mickelson. He clapped his hands. "This is the way to get 'em," he explained. But no servants appeared. The boys were profuse with apologies.

"I don't know what's got into these galoots," said Ed. "But I'll soon find out."

Then three doors opened and the servants emerged, all clad in spotless new white aprons, and all smiling and bowing and seeming greatly honored. The boys looked at them, the cooks looked at the smiling lady, and the dawn came.

"Hey, for Pete's sake!" exclaimed Ed. "You aren't, you can't be, the—the——"

"Oh yes I can be," the lady said, laughing. "I'm the Honorary Commander of the American Volunteer Group. And now we'll really get that tea you promised me."

It was, of course, the First Lady of China, Mei-ling Soong, wife of the Generalissimo, on her way to India for the historic conversations with Nehru and other leaders of the Indian National Congress Party. The "traveling man" whom the Tigers had summarily left at the airdrome was Generalissimo Chiang Kai-shek.

Messrs. Mickelson and Liebolt, after an interim of blushing, apologizing, and stumbling, recovered their poise and turned the hostel inside out to entertain Madame Chiang. Others joined them at tea, and the Tigers purred when their honorary commander told them how much all China appreciated the valiant and valuable service of the men of the A.V.G. That night, before she and the Generalissimo took off for New Delhi, they presented the pilots with their wings as volunteers in the Chinese Air Force.

It was a week of honors, national and international, for

the men of the Group. In London Winston Churchill issued this tribute:

"The magnificent victories they have won in the air over the paddy fields of Burma may well prove comparable in character, if not in scale, with those won over the orchards and the hop fields of Kent in the Battle of Britain.

"To these brave men the thanks of all the United Nations are due," said the British Prime Minister in his message to Major Sir Reginald Hugh Dorman-Smith, governor of Burma.

And Air Vice Marshal D. F. Stevenson, commanding the Royal Air Force in Burma, announced that the "official count" of Japanese planes destroyed by the American Volunteer Group in Burma had reached the hundred mark. That meant that one hundred losses were confirmed by witnesses, or that wreckage of that number of planes had been found. No one doubted that the actual total was closer to two hundred; the evidence lost in the waters of the Gulf of Martaban and in the jungles of Burma and Thailand.

Leland Stowe, in Rangoon for the Chicago *Daily News* foreign service, essayed a breakdown of the results attained by the A.V.G., and reached a total of one hundred and thirty Jap planes as "truly conservative." Of this number, Stowe figured that about forty per cent, or fifty-two planes, were bombers, with crews of from five to eight men each. Striking an average of six and one-half men for each Jap bomber, he placed the Japs' personnel losses in bombers at three hundred and thirty-eight men, plus seventy-eight Jap pilots killed in single-seater fighters, or a total of four hundred and sixteen crew losses for the Japanese.

"In these engagements the A.V.G. lost five pilots killed in action and one believed taken prisoner," wrote Stowe. (One of these, Bert Christman, was "murdered" while descending in his parachute.) "That number of six Americans lost can be placed alongside of more than four hundred Jap airmen who have been wiped out by American fighter pilots in the Burma war theater.

"All feelings of national pride can be put aside in reporting this outstanding and historical achievement of the

A.V.G. in Burma during the last seven weeks. It is an achievement which certainly has very rarely been equalled anywhere since the war began, and possibly not equalled by the same number of airmen operating with ground crews which are very far below the regulation size used by the U.S. Army Air Forces.

"Nevertheless, despite the Nazis' flair for making exorbitant claims for their pilots, even the Germans have never claimed that their squadrons have eliminated enemy air personnel at anything remotely approaching a ratio of six pilots lost against four hundred or more in enemy flying personnel.

"Fortune gave the A.V.G. an opportunity to turn the air war's tide over Burma, but to these young Americans belongs credit for having risen maginficently to an opportunity in which the odds seemed seriously against them."

In that dispatch Leland Stowe was straining for conservatism with both fists. Four hundred-odd against six! Shades of Frank Merriwell, Tom Swift, Tarzan, and Superman! There had never been anything like this since Cain tackled Abel in the first recorded battle of history.

The next day the Tigers started on their second hundred "accredited," with Robert "Buster" Keeton, a former Colorado College fullback, putting the authentic Tiger stripe of spectacularism to the one hundred and first Jap plane. "Buster" was at Toungoo, when he was warned to get his Tomahawk away from an approaching Jap bomber wave. He hurriedly took off without helmet or oxygen equipment. Jap fighters spotted him and chased him up, up, up, to nearly twenty thousand feet, where "Buster" lost consciousness. But on the way down he came to his senses just as a Jap bomber hove into view below him. "Buster" gave the Jap his finishing burst, then coasted down to "John Haig," watching the bomber flaming earthward to its death.

A Tiger's diary records a fight in this period:

"I was coming back from a patrol when I saw a bunch of our boys running for their planes—an alert. I stayed up and joined them. We found fifteen bombers and thirty or so fighters at eighteen thousand feet coming from the

86

southwest. They were approaching that way so they wouldn't have to turn to get back to their base. I was afraid Bob didn't see them so I waggled my wings and started for them, climbing fast. I ignored the bombers and took on four fighters, thinking I had Dick on my wing. In my first run down I caught one fighter with a full burst, and nearly collided with another I was sure I'd hit. Looked back to see if he was on fire—but no, he was chasing me, and no Dick to help me. I tried to maneuver, but it was useless. The two others got on my tail, also, so I dived and came back at them. Never thought about the four to one odds. (Afterward I did, though.) I caught one in my sights and gave him a burst. His plane lurched and fell off in a spiral, smoking. I pulled up sharp to avoid him, and saw two Japs on my tail, firing at me. I half-rolled and spiraled down at full throttle, helpless and hoping they wouldn't get me. A hell of a moment! But I got away. Never could find a Jap when I climbed back. Tonight I felt good about this show. Had been a little afraid I was losing my touch. We're all nervous that way, now and then. They're bombing the ears off this burg tonight. So to bed."

# CHAPTER TWELVE

As the February fighting began the total A.V.G. strength in and around Rangoon was twenty-five battered Tomahawks, only eighteen of which could get into the air at the same time because of lack of replacement parts. The British had only four of their Brewster-Buffalo fighters left, supplemented by ten Hurricane pursuits, a dozen Blenheim bombers and the six antiquated Westland-Lysanders. The Japs inaugurated a new tactic for the daylight raids, sending forces composed approximately of three fighters to each bomber, in the hope that so many fighters could preoccupy the defenders and permit the bombers to go unchallenged to their targets.

In the first of these visitations Bob Sandell and Bob Neale, his vice squadron commander, took their "Adam and Eves" off in two squadrons of five planes each, and met the Japs over the Gulf of Martaban. The Tigers dove from twenty-two thousand feet through the thick screen of fighters onto the back of the bombers cruising below at eight thousand feet. They knocked seven of the bombers into the sea then and there. The other three got through, while the Tigers fought for altitude to get above the swarm of fighters pursuing them. Sandell got two of these on his next trip down, Neale and Charley Bond got their first "certains" of the war. Half of the Jap fighters took after the bombers to protect them after the first melee with the Tigers.

Sandell and his boys got on their tails, leaving Neale, Burgard, Bond, and Bill Bartling to finish the job over the gulf.

The total bag of the day was seven Jap bombers and nine fighters. The last Jap fatality was dramatic in the extreme. As Sandell brought his damaged ship down on Mingaladon the ground crew beckoned to him wildly, directing his attention to the sky. "Sandy" looked and saw a Jap pursuit, with engine sputtering weakly and propeller "wind-milling," heading straight for him with guns firing.

He ran for the ditch and jumped in, and five seconds later the Jap crashed on the runway, shearing off the tail of Sandell's plane. The body of the pilot had been pierced by bullets in the chest, stomach, and head, but he had fought his battle to the last.

The Tigers often discussed the comportment of the Japanese pilots and the bomber crewmen, their blind fidelity to the assignment, their almost inhuman courage, their apparent disregard of death. The bombing crews went straight for their targets, with or without fighter protection, and no matter how many Tigers and R.A.F. fliers came at them. The Japs were like machines, wound up for the occasion, following a mechanized routine of conduct. But when they were separated from their machines and from their fellows, the individual's human weaknesses cropped out. A few Jap fliers had been taken prisoner in Rangoon, and when it was suggested that they might be exchanged for the captured Charley Mott, their toughness melted away and they wailed abjectly. They did not want to return to war, they said. They were happy in jail, explaining that in their defeat and captivity they had lost such "face" that only eternal disgrace or a firing squad could be their fate behind the Japanese lines.

On February sixth the "Panda Bears" escorted the R.A.F. Blenheims on two raids against the Jap land base at Paan, on the Salween, from which the invaders were pointing their attack on Rangoon and the Road. They gave it a thorough pasting, while Newkirk and five others strafed Jap columns moving out from Moulmein, which they had captured a few days before.

The commandant of the Royal Air Force issued special citations on February sixth to Chennault and to Squadron Leaders John Van Kuren Newkirk and Arvid Olson, commenting on the "remarkable fighting qualities" of the Group. It was announced that "Scarsdale Jack" had been recommended for the Distinguished Service Order of the British Empire.

On February sixth with "Sandy" still grounded for repairs, Bob Neale led the Tigers against another huge force of fighters escorting a dozen bombers. They got seven Jap planes without injury to themselves, beyond the usual supplies of lead that punctured their Tomahawks fore and aft in the familiar sieve pattern that decorated every ship in the Group. After they returned to the field and landed most sedately, an American reporter asked why they hadn't indulged in the "victory roll" which formerly had signaled a triumph over the Japs.

"Confidentially," explained Neale, "we can't roll 'em any more. If we tried it, they'd probably fall apart in our laps. At that, if we didn't have the best ground crew on earth right here under Harry Fox, we'd all be sleeping in a nice wet rice paddy."

The February sixth victories saw Neale and "Snuffy" Smith of Eagle River knocking out two victims each, with others being credited to John "Dick" Rossi of San Francisco, Bob Prescott of Fort Worth and Matt Kuykendall of San Saba, Texas.

The next day "Sandy" Sandell took his Tomahawk aloft to test its repairs. The plane went into a spin a few miles from Rangoon and fell, killing the young commander of the "Adam and Eves." His record had been brilliant. New to combat because his squadron came late to the Burma war, he had bagged five Japanese "certains" and several "probables" in his few encounters. "Sandy" came to the A.V.G. from a post as pursuit instructor for the U.S. Army Air Corps at Shreveport, Louisiana. He had been a fiery, inspiring leader and his loss was hard to take.

The command of the First Squadron now passed into the hands of Bob Neale of Seattle, who also assumed direction of all A.V.G. operations thoroughout Burma. Neale was a lanky six-footer with a ready smile who had come from a dive bomber squadron of the U.S.S. *Saratoga* after training at Pensacola Naval Air Training Station. He had never operated a pursuit ship until his arrival in Burma.

At Moulmein, the Japs were only one hundred and sixty land miles from Rangoon. At Paan, only ninety miles separated them from the vital rail line of the Burma Road. They were creeping along the Gulf of Marataban in small boats, and with the fall of Singapore, receiving air and ground reinforcements from Malaya. While the Tigers and R.A.F. boys strafed them and the Imperial forces held them back along the Salween, Generalissimo Chiang Kai-shek flew to New Delhi with Madame Chiang and his generals for staff conferences with General Wavell. The

Chinese leaders conferred also with Pandit Nehru, the new chairman of the Indian National Congress, seeking to establish a solidarity of resistance for the eight hundred millions of Indians and Chinese against the Jap menace. Nehru and the other Hindu nationalists were not encouraging. They wanted self-rule for India as the price for co-operation in the war. But even without a militant Indian population, the Japs seemed due for a licking in Southern Asia. There were nearly a million British troops in India. Chiang promised hundreds of thousands of Chinese man-power, veterans in the task of outwitting and outfighting the Japs. The largest estimate placed upon the Jap invasion force threatening Burma was one hundred thousand men. Most estimates fixed it at fifty thousand including reinforcements from Malaya.

After almost six weeks of continual fighting by day and trying to sleep under the bombs at night, Jack Newkirk, "Tex" Hill and the rest of the Second Squadron were ordered to leave Rangoon for a change of scene on February eighth. Some of them went to Loiwing, others to the new British airdrome at Magwe, and a few to Kunming.

The First Squadron, now alone in Rangoon, had a few quiet days, but on the eleventh they lifted the monotony by escorting the Blenheims to bomb and strafe the docks and troopships of the Japs at Bilin in Burma. A few excerpts from another Tiger's diary illustrate the tempo of life and thought in this period as the storm gathered over Burma.

"February 12. Still no action here. We're deeply puzzled about what the Jap may be cooking up. Evidently they feel they can't cope with the A.V.G. until they increase their fighting force. Five to one isn't a sufficient margin, I guess. But when they bring some of those Navy Zeros up from Singapore, we ought to have lots of fun. But where in hell is the U.S. Army Air Force? Only nine of our wrecks can get off the ground. Four bombs dropped near our window last night, throwing Charley and me clear out of bed. Eight blocks in the neighborhood razed, but we went back to sleep anyway. Thirty-six craters on Mingaladon when we got here this a.m. Oh, for some night fighters! How we could take these babies!

"February 13. I got a day off! Played golf at Mingaladon Club and had a heck of a good time with my caddies—five of them, no less. One bag carrier, one umbrella wielder, two ball spotters, and a guy to fan me! In the p.m. we went swimming at the Kokine Club and acted like rich kids. Busy today preparing for possible evacuation of A.V.G. if Jap ground forces close in. Wonder why they don't send paratroops over? They could finish us at night before we knew what was up. At that, we're almost finished anyway. If we tried to take these planes up for the old U.S. Army or Navy, we'd be courtmartialed and our P-40's would be junked.

"Heard Singapore has fallen. We're all disgusted. Rangoon is certainly a soft touch compared to Singapore. Where, oh where, is the U.S. Army? Where, oh where, is General Wavell? Does the First Squadron of the A.V.G. and a few R.A.F. kids have to handle the whole Japanese invasion?

"February 18. Charley and I are lords of the manor now. The evacuation is on, and we have the Jensen house all to ourselves. The Jensens were swell. They left us their servants and plenty of canned goods. The docks are deserted. The warehouses are wide open and you can pick up anything from a Mack truck to a brand new radio with no one to bother you. The coolies are jamming the roads out of this place. At that, the Transiteers did a great job clearing the lend-lease stuff for China. Somebody brought us a radio. We asked no questions. We got KGEI at San Francisco. It was marvelous.

"February 20. This was 'E' Day, the evacuation of Rangoon. Quite a day. The American Military Mission rounded up everybody who could drive a car, and permitted evacuées to take cars and jeeps northward on their promise to surrender them at Lashio. When the Mission tried to burn up several million lend-lease army blankets destined for China, Col. St. John and Lieut. Wetzel were blown thirty feet by an explosion of gasoline fumes. Only military supplies of secondary importance are being destroyed. They are saving the prime stuff in hopes Rangoon won't fall. It will. Anyway, they invited us to help ourselves, and we got plenty of booze and cigarettes, canned food and a couple of Tommy guns. When they set fire to one *godown* (warehouse) containing twenty thousand cases of Scotch whisky, we knew the end of the world was near. Twenty thousand cases! How many wonderful drunks would that make? No wonder we almost bellered like babies to see it. The dacoits are on the rampage. They're blocking roads with trees and robbing everybody that comes along who is unarmed. We ain't! We've got our .45's, and we show 'em. Understand they killed a couple of Britishers and the Britishers mowed fifty of them down with machine guns. Suits me. The Japs have cut the railroad to Toungoo, so the Burma Road is all washed up at this end. Jap submarines are in the harbor, and their troops only thirty miles from the road to Prome. Our lend-lease trucks are going up that way by the hundreds, with millions of bucks worth of stuff for China, but the British are holding pretty good. Refugees are on top of every truck. We saw to it that all of our friends got away. Then we patrolled above them to make sure they were safe. Lord, I wonder how my darling girl in Mobile is tonight! Think I'll have a peek at her picture.

"February 21. A wild and woolly day. We flew as escort to four Blenheims on a bombing mission and ran smack into 40 Jap fighters and twelve bombers. It was a lucky break but so sudden it scared the pants off us. We were below them and I had to dive out the first time without getting in a shot. There were Japs all over the sky. I tried to shoot them all down myself but only got two in a full hour of fighting. It was a wild scramble. We got six in all before they ran. Johnny Farrell got a bullet through his canopy and I got one through the wing that shot out my right tire. Some fun! Still, we're kind of like wild beasts. Seem to do nothing but eat and sleep and fight. Not so good, not so good. The Japs bombed Mandalay and Maymyo today—plenty! No opposition. Our servants decamped. Don't blame them. Looting and fires all over town. The Japs took Bassein today, and we went on one hour evacuation notice. Just heard that the ground troops and trucks we strafed yesterday were British, not Japs! That British C.O. should be shot, sending us over there. No brains, no intelligence service, no air raid alarm system, no nothing! That strafing killed about one hundred and sixty good game British soldiers—maybe some guys I knew. We all feel terrible about it."

On February twenty-third the panic was on in full force in Rangoon. Neale had received orders to evacuate the ground crew and administration personnel. The A.V.G. convoy started out for Magwe under the command of Dr. Lewis Richards, the well-loved medical officer who had worked so hard and so expertly to keep the guardians of Rangoon in fighting trim. As they took to the road Jim Cross and Johnny Farrell raced up in a truck piled high with crates and packing boxes. Dr. Richards shook his head. The convoy couldn't take any more. But Dr. Richards relented when the cases were opened to reveal hundreds of bottles of Scotch whisky, gin and rum and dry sack. The former owner of this treasure, an American named McCartney, had presented it to the A.V.G. with his compliments on the express condition that they preserve it from the Japs. It could not have found its way to safer hands.

The next day the Tigers strafed Moulmein Airport and got three Jap planes on the ground. General Wavell was quoted as ordering the defense of Rangoon at all costs, but notwithstanding, the R.A.F. took off most of its Blenheims and Hurricanes for Magwe to protect the oil region around Yenangyaung.

On the morning of the twenty-fifth, with the British gone, and the Japs advancing across the Sittang and Salween Rivers, the aerial defense of the great capital of Rangoon was in the hands of eleven pilots and eight crewmen of the "Adam and Eve" Squadron. They stood by for orders from Chennault. The orders read:

"Conserve matériel and personnel. Retire from Rangoon on last bottle of oxygen."

That message was to be famous forever after in the A.V.G. The matériel consisted of seven tomahawks, patched, old, and overworked. The flight personnel was composed of Bob Neale, Charley Bond, George Burgard, Bill McGarry, Jim Cross, Bob Prescott, Ed Liebolt, Dick Rossi, Bill Bartling, Johnny Blackburn of Amarillo, new to the wars, and Bob Little of Spokane. Eleven weary fliers, seven worn airplanes, the Jap juggernaut just around the corner, and coming fast.

The Tigers assembled in the "ready" shack an hour before dawn, to plot the day's work. Their plight appeared so desperate, their resources so ludicrously scant, that the whole situation overlapped from the serious into the comic.

Bob Prescott struck the keynote, when he grinned and said:

"There's only one thing for us guys to do now. I say let's declare open war on the Empire of Japan."

Twenty minutes before dawn flashes in the dark sky and cracks of thunder announced the final night bombing raids on Rangoon and the Road. The bombs continued to fall after sun-up, indicating the Japs' confidence that they had seen the last of the Flying Tigers.

Neale maintained constant patrols in the air through the morning, as the Rangoon telephone warning net was now non-existent. The A.V.G. had a British radio detector device, but this instrument had also been to the wars too long, and was prone to collapse at crucial periods. About noon the Japs came over with thirty new Zero fighters and a dozen bombers. Only three Tigers got into the air before the invader appeared, but these knocked down four Jap fighters and kept the bombers away. The Japs put up very little fight, apparently content with having measured the defending force, but at five o'clock that evening they came over in earnest, forty bombers and twenty fighters strong. The Tigers had plenty of notice and every one of the seven planes was waiting in the sun. They had a field day. Neale got four "certains" and on "probable," his high mark for the war, "Snuffy" Smith, Bond, and Burgard got three apiece, while other of the Japs fell to the marksmanship of Jim Rossi, Bill McGarry, Bill Bartling, Bob Little, John Blackburn, Joe Rosbert, and Bob Prescott. Two Tigers were missing; Ed Liebolt and husky Jim Cross. They waited, hoping they might have chased some Japs and would turn up soon. After an hour a car drove up and out stepped a figure in flight overalls, covered with blood, his face as yellow as a lemon.

It was Jim. The medical officer hurried him to a rough board bed and started digging shrapnel pieces from his head and shoulders. The boys gathered anxiously around for Jim's report.

"I made the mistake of taking on the most popular boy in the Jap air force, I guess," said Jim. "Soon as I went for him fifteen of his friends ganged up on me."

But despite his wounds Jim had brought his precious Tomahawk down safely on John Haig field, and the Tigers

95

still possessed a seven plane "armada." Their score that day was twenty-three "certains," while the R.A.F. reported six, the total of twenty-nine making it a record-breaking calamity for Japanese military aviation. But Ed Liebolt was still missing as night fell.

All that night the Japs bombed the Rangoon area with unprecedented fury. The Tigers were on the alert at dawn, and when no Japs appeared, Neale decided to pay them a visit. He and seven others headed for the Jap base at Moulmein. Approaching the city they saw three Jap pursuits on an auxiliary field. The Tigers attacked and left two of them in flames. Hurrying to the main airdrome, they caught three Jap pursuits preparing to take off and twenty others warming up. Neale, Rossi, and Burgard, flying in front, dove at once. Rossi and Burgard got their victims but Neale missed his man, who wheeled directly in front of Burgard at four hundred feet. This Jap fell an easy victim to a short burst. Other Tigers descended on the field with Bond, Little, and Rosbert remaining above for "top cover." Suddenly a cloud of Japs appeared from the south and the Tigers forsook their strafing to take on the active foe. It was a field day, for everyone except Bob Neale. Three of the Japs got on his tail and he went speeding out over the Gulf of Martaban, with bullets splattering into his instrument panel and windshield and tail. Forty miles out Bob found a lush cloudbank at a thousand feet altitude, ran into it and played hide and seek until the Japs gave up the search for him. He got back to John Haig safely, with sixteen bullet holes in his plane but none in himself.

The other fellows had done nobly, "Snuffy" Smith topping the day's score with three Jap fighters to his list; Bill McGarry got two, as did George Burgard, and Charley Bond, Little and Blackburn one each. For Jack Blackburn it was his second flight, and his second Jap.

With eleven in the bag, and no losses, the Tigers felt like rest and food. But there was no food, and the Japs saw to it that they had no rest. They came in volume for revenge early in the afternoon, twenty bombers and fifteen fighters, but the Tiger patrol spotted them well out and as they approached Rangoon seven Tomahawks were waiting in the sun. The first dive got two Japs, so did the second, and when the third attack made it seven, even the stoical Japs

Latest U.S. Government
tests of all cigarettes
show True is
lower in both
tar and nicotine
than 99% of all other
cigarettes sold.

Think about it.
Shouldn't your next cigarette be True?

Regular and Menthol: 12 mg. "tar," 0.7 mg. nicotine,
av. per cigarette, FTC Report Apr. '72.

Latest U.S. Government
tests of all menthol
cigarettes show
True is lower
in both tar and
nicotine than 99% of
all other menthols sold.

Think about it.
Shouldn't your next cigarette be True?

Warning: The Surgeon General Has Determined That
Cigarette Smoking Is Dangerous to Your Health.

© Lorillard 1972

figured they had enough. Bob Prescott and Dick Rossi added a fighter apiece for good measure as the Japs were leaving, making it twenty for the "Adam and Eves" that day. During the day the boys had taken every opportunity to search for Ed Liebolt, but the jungle yielded no sign of him or his plane. Except for Ed's loss, they had obeyed the first sentence of Chennault's classic order: "Conserve matériel and personnel . . ." But their instructions were to "retire on the last bottle of oxygen." The last bottles had been well drained.

That night the Tigers buckled on their side-arms for a last look at "Hometown," their radio code name for Rangoon. They saw a shambles and a horror. From a hundred fires a great pall of black smoke stretched across the sky. Wharves, factories, rice and teak mills, oil storage plants, vessels in the river and homes and buildings in the town were in flames. In the streets lay hundreds of bodies of Indians who had fallen in the pogrom declared by the Burmese against these resented foreigners when doom closed down upon Rangoon. Over these bodies stumbled ragged, bedlamite bands of looters and rioters, loosed from the jails and asylums when the attendants deserted their posts. Here were imbeciles, maniacs, criminals, cripples, victims of every disease of mind and body known to the East. They roamed the city, shrieking in crazy choruses, throwing burning brands into the windows of buildings, destroying and desecrating. The smells of Rangoon were now the smells of embers and of death.

About the famous Shwe Dagon pagoda with its priceless jeweled Buddhas and its sheath of gold, the priests in their orange robes stood guard against flame and vandal. But lesser temples fell to the looters and the firebugs, whose lust made the originally half-hearted "scorched earth" policy of the British an almost complete success.

The Tigers had seen danger and death before. But these were scenes no man should look upon. It was a saturnalia without joy. But perhaps it was a fitting tribute to the gods of war.

## CHAPTER THIRTEEN

In these final Rangoon battles the Tigers had destroyed not less than forty-three Japanese airplanes with the loss of a single man and a single Tomahawk. Ed Liebolt had bailed out near Moulmein, and, they guessed, was now a prisoner of war. His loss was the one shadow upon the greatest two-day execution the Tigers had wrought in two months of fighting. Ed was a likable fellow and a fine pilot. He had made himself famous in the A.V.G. for the tea party given to Madame Chiang at Kunming early in February.

Final evacuation began. The ground crew under Harry Fox started northward in touring cars and trucks, with the Tigers guarding them from above. This ground crew of nine men had won the eternal gratitude of all the Tigers during that last game stand at Rangoon. Night and day they had worked amid bombings and strafings to get the Tomahawks back into action. These men were: Ed McClure of San Diego, Frank Jacobson of Racine, Wisconsin, Bob Rasmussen of Omaha, Nebraska, J. J. Harrington of Dothan, Alabama, J. B. Carter of Lafayette, Louisiana, J. L. Overley of Denver, Colorado, R. J. Neale of Greene, Iowa, Willis Shafer of Chicago, Illinois, and Irving Gove, of Simsbury, Connecticut—nine brave boys.

Most of the Tigers took off for Magwe early in the afternoon of February twenty-eighth. Neale and "Snuffy" Smith got away late, lost Magwe in the overcast, but fortunately survived forced landings north of the city.

In Magwe they were besieged by newspaper correspondents for the details of their last heroic battles at Rangoon. "Snuffy" Smith explained it thus:

"We had more fun than you could shake a stick at. Nothing to it. We just sat up there in the sun and picked off the Japs as they came in. But gosh, if we'd had Kittyhawks or Republic or Vultee fighters, how much easier it would have been. If we can knock 'em off with our Tomahawks when they have a climbing speed and maneuverability superior to ours, what wouldn't we do with newer, better ships of our own."

"Snuffy" gave the press a statement for the American people.

"I don't want to sound stuffy," said "Snuffy," "but here's the dope; it's a lot of baloney about us being the kind of guys who'll win this war. All we can do is fight with what the folks at home give us to fight with. I'll tell you the people who can do more than any others to win this thing—that's the workers in every factory in the old U.S.A.

"If they'll turn out the planes—planes just as good as anything the Japs and Germans have—we'll really begin to hang up some records. And when they get us a ship just a shade better, I just want to be there. Oh, that's going to be a barrel of fun, I'm telling you.

"But it can't come too soon. I hope to God the folks back home know how much it would mean to us out here."

The dashing commander of the First, Bob Neale, already the leading ace of the A.V.G. with fourteen "confirmed" Jap planes to his list and many more "probables," characteristically gave a large share of the credit for the Rangoon victories to the men of the ground crew. He ticked off the names and home towns of the men, and said:

"Be sure to mention their names, will you? We guys who fly 'em have been getting too much of the glory. Why, these boys of ours are so good they'd have got us into the air in wheelbarrows if they had to."

A British aircraftsman named Johnny Morrison spoke up:

"Let me get in my tuppenny worth," said Johnny. "I've seen these Volunteers all through the Rangoon trouble. They're the greatest air fighters the world has ever seen. Five to one, ten to one, they don't count the odds. They cut 'em down to their size every time. And those airplanes they flew—why, I wouldn't take a ride in one of them on a pleasure cruise if you gave me Buckingham Palace."

Johnny was silver gray at thirty-five. He had been many places in the war, and now the A.V.G. had brought him along from Rangoon in one of their trucks. He accosted a Tiger that afternoon.

"I want to tell you a story, Yank," he said. "I was at

Dunkirk and they left me on the beach. I made me a raft while the Jerries strafed, and floated her out at night 'til a trawler found me. Then later on they left me at Crete and I set to sea with a log for company. Some Greek fishermen picked me up that time. Now you saw the colonel fly off and leave me at Rangoon. Well, I want to quit his war. I want to fight with you. You've got the grandest outfit in the world."

But Johnny's offer of service had to be refused.

One of the reporters wanted to know why Chennault, their commander, had not directed the defense of Rangoon in person.

"If we'd needed the 'Old Man,' he'd have been there," a Tiger explained. "You can bet on that. And one of the reasons we do so well is because he trusts us. He showed us how to fight the Japs. Then he delegated authority to the right men. We like the responsibility. He knows we like it, and when he's satisfied with our ability, he gives us our heads. Take it from me, he's the old master. A hard guy, sure. But you've got to be hard to fight this man's war."

Rangoon fell on March seventh, with five Tigers covering the retreat of the last demolition squads. The "post-mortems" on Rangoon were many. It was generally agreed that the defense had been botched from first to last, except in the air, where the A.V.G. and the R.A.F. had given the Japs all they could handle. There was one other favorable note: the Prome Road had been kept open until the last. Caravans of lend-lease material for China got through to the North. But millions of dollars' worth of military essentials had been destroyed or abandoned, nevertheless. And again China's access to the sea was lost.

The men of the "Adam and Eves" missed the big event in the A.V.G. hostel at Kunming the night of February twenty-eighth, but their exploits at Rangoon were toasted jubilantly in the wines of China and the juice of Scotland. The hosts were the Generalissimo and Madame Chiang, and the Volunteers of the Second and Third Squadrons had the opportunity to study the two illustrious leaders of the new China. The "Madame" they adored. She was fine, fragile, womanly, and the nobility of her spirit commanded the room. She spoke their own language better than they did themselves. They felt for her deep respect, mellowed

100

with brotherliness. The Generalissimo was a different article. Here was a king among men, as "Madame" was a queen. There was no mistaking his kingship. The head needed no crown, the slim body in its plain khaki needed no trappings of royalty. Chiang Kai-shek was what his dreams and deeds had made him, one of the great of history. The Volunteers were accustomed to taking their banquets lightly and damply. But this night, there was no banter, no horseplay. They knew where they were.

The Generalissimo rose to speak. He spoke in Chinese, but they listened to every word, not understanding one in fifty. They were listening to the spirit—the spirit that inspired and led one-fifth of all the people in the world. And then an interpreter told them what Chiang had said:

"To be with you American volunteers here today, to observe your excellent spirit and to hear of your achievements fills me with delight and admiration. The American Volunteer Group of the Chinese Air Force has acquired a worldwide reputation for greatest courage.

"It is three months since the Japanese, our common enemy, picked their quarrel with Great Britain and the United States. The splendid victories the Volunteer Group has won in the air are a glory that belongs to China and our ally, America, alike.

"I have already communicated the news of your repeated successes to your Government and President Roosevelt. The record of what you have done shows that every one of you has been a match for thirty or more of the enemy. Your friends and relations will undoubtedly have felt boundless pride and elation to hear of your exploits. The blows you have struck at the Japanese have put you in the forefront of the Allied forces fighting the aggressor. You have established a firm foundation for the campaign against lawlessness which China and America are united to wage. You have written in the history of this world war a remarkable page, the memory of which will live in our minds forever.

"As the Supreme Commander of the Allied Forces operating in the China theater of war I am entertaining you today as my comrades-in-arms and on behalf of my four hundred and fifty million fellow countrymen I salute you, confident that you will continue together with all the Allied forces in Burma to display your valor until final victory is won over our common enemy.

"Since you are under my command I wish to impress upon you your identity with all the other men serving in the Chinese armed forces. Your lives are one with theirs and mine, your good name is one with theirs and mine. I act toward you as I act toward other members of the Chinese Air Force. I shall extend to those of your comrades who have given their lives the same mark of distinction and the same care for their families and children. For this I hold myself responsible. I trust that you will perform your duties free from any anxiety on this score. Your task is great. When victory is ours I hope to celebrate together with you our successful issue of the war in Tokyo."

It was a proud moment for Claire L. Chennault when he rose to respond to the Generalissimo. In nine weeks his little volunteer air force had become world-famed. It had achieved miracles of heroism, of endurance, and in results. It had proved his point: given the right kind of men and planes he could wallop the Jap every time. But characteristically, he did not speak of his triumph. He talked about the Chinese, and their leaders who now were hosts to the A.V.G.

"Never before in history," said Chennault, "do I know of any military unit such as ours having been accorded the honor that comes to us tonight. No matter how many decorations we may have bestowed on us in the future I am sure we will never receive more honor than we have received tonight. For five years I have followed the Generalissimo to the best of my ability and I know him to be a leader of the highest principles and greatest determination. He is a leader who prefers death to compromise. He is a leader not only of China but of the entire Allied effort. It is easy for us Americans to follow such a leader.

"In addition to Madame Chiang's work in aviation she is also the leader of all the women in China. The orphans and widows of China come to her either directly or through the agencies which she has set up and all receive aid. To me, she is the mother of China.

"During this time millions of Chinese soldiers have gone to the fronts and have been killed and seriously wounded. Orphans have been left in the ruins of their homes and in the fields. All of these need aid and they have been given that aid as rapidly as possible. And now there will be thousands more to feed and educate, to receive medical attention. I would be unable to recite all that Madame Chiang had accomplished, however, one thing I have not yet mentioned. When the organization of this Group was first discussed in America I was asked for recommendations as to how it would be handled in China. The first thing that I insisted upon was that Madame Chiang would act as our chief staff officer. Madame Chiang would serve as liaison staff officer between the Generalissimo and the Group. And although she has hundreds of activities that require a great deal of her time she consented to this because of her eagerness for China to have an effective military aviation. So Madame Chiang has been Honorary Group Commander and Staff Officer of this Group since its organization and I would like to present her tonight as our Honorary Group Commander."

The boys hailed Madame Chiang vociferously, as she rose to speak. She smiled happily, and said:

"As your Honorary Commander may I call you my boys? You have flown across the Pacific in China's gravest hour on wings of hope and faith. For this reason not only the Chinese Air Force but the entire Chinese nation welcomes you with outstretched arms. The Generalissimo has already spoken to you of the fine and brave deeds you have done and he has called the A.V.G. the world's bravest air force.

"I am very proud tonight that I have had a little share in making it possible for you to fight for China. When I think of the life-and-death struggle which China has passed through this last five years I have before my mind's eye the millions of our people who have been killed or wounded and others who had to flee from Japanese cannon, machine guns and bombers. I also see the rivers of blood which have flowed over our territory, the very life blood of China's fairest manhood. I think of the tens of thousands of our women whose honor has been violated by the Japanese and the hundreds of thousands of our little children who have been killed and maimed or else taken to Japan to be trained as traitors to their motherland.

"And now you have come here to vindicate us. We have

103

always been resolved to fight until final victory is ours but we lack the air arm which you are now providing. You have come to fight side by side with us. For this I wish to express our heartfelt thanks.

"Colonel Chennault has taken an active part in Chinese resistance during the last five years. You boys know him personally. You know what an admirable commander he is and how very selfless. The only complaint I have against him is that he is never satisfied with his own work. I venture to say, too, that he also thinks that you ought to have more work regardless of how much you already have.

"Colonel Chennault has just introduced me as Honorary Commander of the A.V.G. I think I am prouder of this title than any other title I've had, because I know that you are not only fighting with your bodies and your skill, you are fighting with your hearts and spirits. Just now Colonel Chennault brought to me two of your very fine comrades who have braved death today in the air. They forgot themselves entirely while fighting the enemy because they know that although they might have to make the final sacrifice their comrades would carry on the great work which the A.V.G. has set for itself. This spirit, I feel, is the secret of the A.V.G.'s successes.

"I was asked a little while ago by one of my officers, 'Madame Chiang, some of the A.V.G. pilots are shooting down so many planes that we won't have room enough on the wings for all the stars which they merit. What shall we do about it?' I told him, 'We shall have to provide them with an additional pair of wings.' And this is what we will have to do if you all keep up the score.

"Although you are here in China I am sure that often your minds and your hearts fly back to your loved ones in America, and for this reason I am very glad that America is now realizing that China is not fighting for China alone but for America and for the whole world. You, in giving the best that is in you, are doing it for your own country as well as for China. Time and again your Commanding Officer has dinned into your ears the necessity for discipline on the field, and yet without discipline we can accomplish nothing and I, as your Honorary Commanding Officer, am going to din more discipline into you.

"I would go further than Colonel Chennault. I mean the

discipline of your inner selves. It isn't enough to observe outward discipline only. We must have inner discipline so that we may have fully developed characters. However, I am not trying to make you little saints, but I do want you boys to remember one thing: the whole of the Chinese nation has taken you to its heart and I want you to conduct yourselves in a manner worthy of the great traditions that you have built up. I want you to leave an impression on my people, a true impress of what Americans really are. I trust and I know that you will act worthily wherever you are in China.

"Forgive me for speaking to you like that . . . But you are my boys. I can speak to you freely. I know that you will understand when I say that I hope every one of you, whether in the air or on the ground, will remember that you are China's guests and that everything you do will reflect credit upon the country which I love next to my own, America, where as you know I was educated and which I always look upon as my second home . . .

"Just one final word. War is not only a matter of equipment, artillery, ground troops or air force; it is largely a matter of spirit, or morale. When I came into this room I felt at once how very keyed up you are. Now that you have been fighting for a few months you are full of enthusiasm and pep. That is a good thing but the greater thing is to gather momentum as each day goes by and not let yourself be discouraged no matter what happens, because as you soar into the skies you are writing in letters of flame on the horizon certain eternal truths for the world to see: First: The indomitable courage of the Chinese people, Second: The indestructible spirit of the Chinese Army, and Third: The deathless soul of the Chinese nation. And so, whatever you do, wherever you are remember that such is the China which you have come to assist.

"I would like all of you to get up and drink a toast to the two great sister nations of both sides of the Pacific. They now have a bond of friendship and sympathy which serves us well in the crucible of war and which will serve us equally when victory has been won."

Before the banquet decorations of the Order of the Cloud Banner had been given many of the Tigers, including posthumous awards to Bob "Sandy" Sandell and Louis

Hoffman. Other recipients of this Chinese honor were Ken Jernstedt, Fritz Wolf of Shawano, Wisconsin, "Duke" Hedman, Ed Overend, Charley Older, Parker Dupouy, Arvid Olson, Tom Haywood, and George McMillan. Bob Neale and Bob Little had been recommended for the Distinguished Flying Cross of the British Empire for their work with the "Adam and Eves" at Rangoon.

Many of the Second and Third Squadron pilots went to India and Africa late in February and early in March in transport planes to bring back thirty new P-40 E's (Kittyhawks) which had been landed at Accra on the Gold Coast. Reinforcements at last! The boys left in Kunming and Lashio envied these assignments, and waited eagerly for the new ships, which carried six .50 caliber machine guns in the wings and were reputedly faster than the P-40 B's that had served them so well for so long.

As March began the battle for Asia and the Pacific was going badly on many fronts. Sumatra with its wealth of tin and oil was falling; the Japs were bombing Bali and Darwin, and applying the pincers of sky and surface attack on Java.

The immediate job that concerned the A.V.G. was to help keep the Japs out of upper Burma. Through the mountains to the northeast one hundred thousand Chinese were laboring to repeat the miracle of the lost Burma Road. This new prospective lifeline of China was pointed from Sichang to Sidaya in India, across ten thousand foot high peaks. But the titanic task was far from finished.

At last Chinese troops, veterans of four and one half years of war, were pouring through Lashio on their way to grips with the oncoming Japs. History perhaps will tell why those Chinese armies were held so long near the northern frontier, while the invader slithered through the jungles and captured the rivers of southern and eastern Burma.

Wavell and General Lewis Brereton of the U.S. Army Air Forces conferred in Lashio with the Generalissimo and Chennault. The Tigers, awaiting the repair of their ships and the next battle, slept late and long, swam in the Irrawaddy and wondered how the British could drink lime squash without ice.

None of the new P-40 E's had yet arrived, when two aerial miscarriages grounded half the Group.

In the first of these, five Tomahawks cracked up two hundred miles from Kunming after escorting the transport plane taking the Generalissimo, Madame Chiang and their staff to Chungking. The pilots got back safely, after varied experiences with Chinese natives who mistook them for Japs, but their planes were not repaired and returned for some time. Two days later five Tigers from the Third Squadron got lost in the haze trying to find Loiwing, and had forced and forcible landings. With ten Tomahawks put out of commission in forty-eight hours, the strength of the A.V.G. was low indeed, and the Colonel's temper correspondingly high.

# CHAPTER FOURTEEN

There stood in Lashio an English signboard which most of the A.V.G. had seen, indicating distances to various of the world's capitals. To the westward, it stated, New York was 10291 miles away; to the eastward, 12923 miles. Anyway, America was a long way off, and it was difficult to maintain touch with families and friends back home across a world at war.

A month, two months, might pass without any letters from America. Then a big batch, accumulated or lost somewhere for a period of weeks, would arrive and send the lucky recipient to a quiet spot to devour the news from home. Relatives wrote the usual warm human stuff, about the new baby next door, and the younger brother getting along fine in high school, and the family dog's adventures, and the neighbors who wanted to know how things went in Asia. Invariably the letters wound up with the complaint familiar to all boys away from home: "Why on earth don't you write once in a while?" The boys did write pretty faithfully, but ten thousand miles is ten thousand miles in any direction, and in between were wars and sinking ships and the upheaval of whole civilizations. So when complaints arrived the men of the A.V.G. took to the radiogram. It cost a few dollars but it was worth it in quieting the fears of their loved ones.

At forty cents a word the radiograms were not verbose. One of the master works of condensation was achieved by Frank Lawlor in a message to his young wife and baby son Lindsay in San Diego. Wrote Frank:

"Shot four Japs. Is Lindsay walking?"

Their messages and letters were dearly treasured. Proudly their families displayed them to solicitous friends; proudly the home town newspapers printed their every word, and then dragged out the adjective box to elaborate on the experiences and exploits of the local boy off soldiering in the Orient. Some of the fellows had been born in one town, and grown to manhood in another. Both towns claimed the absent hero in the fierce competition of headlines. Other resourceful editors printed interviews with citizens who had known the Volunteer before fame wreathed him with laurel. Bob Neale's former boss in the Northern Pacific roundhouse at Yakima, Washington, stated for the record that "Bob was as expert at mopping up locomotives as he is at mopping up Japs." Editors and interviewees expatiated on the boundless virtues the home town hero had always possessed. Months later the fading clippings would reach the subject "somewhere in Asia." They gave the boys great joy. They couldn't get enough of them. But one of the Tigers made a tactical blunder in flaunting a home town editorial which acclaimed "our shining knight of the air, Fighting Billy——." For weeks thereafter Billy endured such remarks as "Will the shining knight of the air please pass the beans?"

The letters from home were brave. They tried to hide the sadness and the fear; the longing of the girl left behind; they did not tell of the misty eyes of Dad and Mother sitting under the lamp in the living room, studying the oft-thumbed snapshots of their boy, and placing his messages and news items in the brand new scrapbook with the silver airplane embossed on its cover.

The dark sorrow came to those families that received the radiogram from Chennault announcing the death of a Volunteer and expressing the sympathy of the Group. Soon after, a letter from Washington, which read:

"Dear ————

"It is with deep regret that I have learned of the death of your son ————

"He was one of a group of brave and farsighted young men who sensed the danger not only to China, but to America and to freedom throughout the world, in the ruthless and predatory course of Japanese militarism. Not waiting to be called, this group went forward to meet the enemy, prepared to sacrifice themselves, if need be, in order that the democracies might gain precious time, that freedom might live, that countless other lives might be saved.

"The record already made by the American Volunteer Group in aerial combat against the Japanese is one of which every American may be proud. Although this may be of small comfort to you, in view of your son's sacrifice, perhaps it will help you to feel that he met death as I am sure he would have wanted to meet it—in valiant action against an enemy not only of China, but also of his own country.

"You may have heard that the American Volunteer Group has adopted, as its emblem, a 'Flying Tiger.' The figure chosen was designed by the Walt Disney Studios, and shows a winged tiger leaping out of a Victory 'V.' It will be worn as a lapel insignia by your son's comrades and will also appear in color on the fuselage of each plane. As a tribute to your son's memory, I have the honor to send you, under separate cover, a gold replica of the insignia which he so richly deserved.

"As Foreign Minister of the Republic of China, I want to express to you on behalf of my countrymen and of Generalissimo Chiang Kai-shek personally, the sense of honor which is ours that your son saw fit to give his life in China for the cause of freedom. Like Lafayette in America, these gallant young men will ever be gratefully enshrined in the memory of the Chinese people."

"Very truly yours,
(Signed) T. V. Soong"
"Minister for Foreign Affairs
of the Republic of China"

And finally, a letter from the Rev. Paul Frillman, of Maywood, Illinois, chaplain of the A.V.G., giving the details of the death and telling the bereaved that the clothes and other possessions of the lost son would be carefully protected and returned. These messages joined the others in the new scrapbook. They were the last entries.

At dawn on March nineteenth Bill Reed of Marion, Iowa, and Ken Jernstedt of Yamhill, Oregon, went traveling to observe Jap troop concentrations and movements to the southward. In the flare chutes of their Tomahawks they carried a number of thirty-pound incendiary and fragmentation bombs, a most unusual, if not an entirely unprecedented experiment which Chennault had decided to try. Bill and Ken sneaked along through the clouds over the air base at Moulmein, and sighted twenty-five Jap planes being prepared for the day's work. They dove at once and raked the line with machine-gun fire, then came back and dropped their little eggs. The results were startling. Several of the Jap ships disintegrated into splinters, a dozen others burst into flames. The Tigers, getting away, counted fifteen utterly destroyed out of twenty-five. This figure was confirmed by British observation planes later in the morning.

The use of light bombs by speedy, low-flying fighter planes against ground positions had often been discussed by students of military aviation. Its proponents argued that fragmentation bombs, bursting on impact with the ground, might easily do as much damage to a closely packed target of planes or troops as would a much heavier and more expensive demolition bomb. The two Tigers proved the theory once and forever at Moulmein.

The novel foray on Moulmein had one other repercussion. The Governor of Jernstedt's home state of Oregon radioed a message to Ken, expressing pride in his achievements, deploring the Tigers' scanty equipment, and asking him to name the kind of airplane the home folks should buy and send over to him in Burma.

At Magwe the British and American army engineers were striving to construct an Allied air base that, given a sizable complement of planes, might command the sky over upper and central Burma and in time help turn the tide of war against the Japs. Work was going forward at a fast pace and it was understood that British and American air forces in India would be moved in as soon as accommodations were ready.

But the Japs moved in first. With only a minute's warning ten Jap bombers and twenty fighters came over the field on March twenty-first, and as the first bombs dropped, three of the Tigers and two R.A.F. boys managed to get their "cold" planes into the air. Before they could engage the Japs another wave of twenty bombers with fighter "cover" came over and let loose their loads. As great explosions rocked the airfield and buildings, Bill Reed and Parker Dupouy headed for a convoy of seven Zeros. Parker dived on the most laggard of these and it blew up scarcely fifty yards in front of him. Reed, wounded by shrapnel in his first attack and almost blinded, had to dive out of the

111

fight. The other six Japs turned on Parker, who caught slugs in the legs and arms and had to follow Reed down to what safety there was amid the inferno on the field. Jernstedt, attacking ten bombers in close formation, was also wounded and forced to withdraw.

A third wave of the assault numbering some twenty bombers next appeared over the field.

Cowering in staggered trenches along the edge of Magwe airdrome, the grounded A.V.G. and R.A.F. could only wait, and hope, and take the fearful assault. As fires broke out in headquarters buildings and among the parked airplanes, and bombs tore huge holes in the field, a British Hurricane came racing down for a landing. The wheels hit, ran along a few yards, struck a shallow hole, and the plane careened and nosed over. The pilot could be seen slumped over in the cockpit. Pilot Frank N. Swartz of Dunmore, Pennsylvania, one of the "Hell's Angels," clambered out of the trench to rescue the stricken R.A.F. boy, followed by John Fauth of Red Lion, Pennsylvania, a crew chief, and Bill Seiple, a mechanic. Just then a bomb exploded near by, and the three Americans fell flat on their faces, wounded by shrapnel and smashed by the concussion. Dr. Lewis Richards climbed out of his trench, picked up Swartz and carried him to a jeep parked close by, then assisted others in dragging Fauth and Seiple back to the trench, just as Jap fighters in a wide row came down to strafe the field. In the face of this withering onslaught Doc "Rich" piloted Swartz in the jeep across the ruined airfield to the hospital. The young Tiger had been badly hit.

The Japs completed their carnival of destruction with no opposition except some ineffectual anti-aircraft fire. When they had departed, the men of the A.V.G. and the R.A.F. crawled out of their holes and fought the fires in the planes and buildings. The runway was a series of craters. Six Tomahawks and eight Hurricane fighters seemed beyond repair. Three of the Blenheims had been blown up with their loads of bombs, and eight others were almost utterly destroyed. As the men struggled to save the few remaining planes several delayed action bombs exploded, starting new fires.

Magwe was a scene of ruin when the smoke and dust finally cleared. Amid heaps of ashes lay twisted motors and the charred wings and fuselages of half the aerial strength of the United Nations in Burma.

Frank Swartz and Bill Seiple were flown to Calcutta in an ambulance plane. John Fauth died of his wounds the next morning. Frank died two months later.

On the following day four of the Tigers took their planes for safety's sake to Loiwing, leaving Dupouy, Jernstedt, Rossi, and Prescott at Magwe. While the British and A.V.G. ground crews were at work on the damaged ships, a great cloud of Jap bombers appeared without warning and again rained their hellfire on the field. This time they had no opposition whatsoever. Not a Tiger could reach his plane. Only a few of the British got into the air and these fell to the assault of over-whelming numbers of Jap fighters. The airdrome and its buildings were put right out of the war by hundreds of demolition bombs. After the Japs departed the A.V.G. piled its five remaining P-40's onto trucks—none of them had escaped damage—and evacuated to Loiwing. The R.A.F. retreated into India with the few planes it could salvage. That was the last of Magwe. Thereafter, the Japs blasted the cities of northern Burma almost without challenge. The Chinese and British forces were left without hope of aerial protection against strafing and bombing. The report that the British C.O. in charge at Magwe would be court-martialed for failure to provide either a warning net or radio detector reached the A.V.G. in Loiwing. No dissent was voiced there. The officer concerned was known throughout Burma as "The Killer" for the murderous risks to which he had subjected the R.A.F. pilots under his command.

At Kunming the Tigers plotted to make payment in kind for the blow the Japs had dealt the United Nations at Magwe. At Chiengmai in central Thailand the enemy had its strongest air base on the continent of Asia. That was the target selected. On the afternoon of March twenty-third Neale took five of the First Squadron down to an auxiliary field at Nam Sang, where they slept under the wings of their Tomahawks after fueling up for a pre-dawn departure.

It was arranged that they would make a rendezvous with Newkirk and three others from the Second Squadron near Chiengmai shortly after daybreak on the twenty-fourth, but for once the famous teamwork of the A.V.G. slipped a cog.

When the "Adam and Eves" reached the designated point there was no sign of the "Panda Bears." Far down below Neale saw the strafer's dream, fifty Jap ships drawn up close together in long even rows. But apparently warned of the proximity of the Tigers, the field suddenly swarmed with pilots and crewmen preparing the planes for flight. There was no time to wait for any of the others. Bob barked into his radio:

"Neale to all pilots! McGarry and Rector get to twenty thousand feet and cover us from the top. Bond and Boyington and Bartling follow me to strafe. On the first pass hit them from north to south. Let's go, you birds!"

Bartling yelled back:

"Bart to Neale! Watch the south end of the field. It's loaded with machine-gun nests."

The four Tigers started down. At twelve thousand feet they ran through a hail of anti-aircraft, the worst they had ever encountered. Their first blazing pass caught the Japs still on the ground and the hunting was good. With machine gun and rifle bullets slapping into their Tomahawks they roared back on the dangerous errand of the second pass.

Flames were already leaping from the Jap ships and spreading to others. The second strafing fired a few more and as the Tigers wheeled for the third pass, the radio spoke:

"McGarry to Neale! We're coming down, Skipper. I want to try a couple of those monkeys for size!"

There was no use trying to keep "Black Mac" out of the fight. Neale, Bond, and the others drove back through the cruel ground fire in their third pass, followed by McGarry and Rector with all guns blazing. At least twenty Jap ships were burning as the Tigers finished their run and turned to survey the job. Most of the others had been riddled with red-hot lead.

"Neale to all pilots! Knock off and beat it for home. Rendezvous at Point A as planned. That's all!"

With the "ack-ack" bursting around them they gave their Tomahawks the gun, but when they gained altitude the others saw that McGarry's plane was spouting smoke. They questioned Mac by radio.

"I'm okay, boys. A little trouble but I'll make it if I go easy. You guys keep going."

But they stayed near him, and soon it was apparent that Mac's Tomahawk was faltering. Mac yelled:

"This crate is going to quit on me. I can't keep her up. Give me a check on my position and when I lose all the altitude I can afford, I'll hit the silk."

Bond answered him:

"Charley to Mac. We're about fifty-five miles from the border. When you land head northwest steadily. You can make the Salween River that way and we'll have Chinese troops out looking for you. Good luck, Mac. See you soon."

With smoke streaming out behind his ship McGarry called back:

"Okay, kid. Position checks. My oil pressure is all gone, so I'll be leaving you now."

The others watched Black Mac as he put his Tomahawk gracefully into a half-roll, and dropped out. His 'chute opened quickly and he drifted down into a clearing in the valley. As they circled above they saw Mac land easily, fold up his 'chute and start through the woods, straight northwest.

The "Adam and Eves," at the moment, felt certain that Mac would get home safely. Their worry concerned "Scarsdale Jack" and the others of the Second Squadron.

Newkirk and his men, missing the "Adam and Eves" at the rendezvous, had put on all power and raced toward Chiengmai. Their assignment was to search for "satellite" fields and to prevent any planes they might find thereon from going to the defense of the main Jap air base. Finding no evidence of Jap ships they headed for the big target. On the way they strafed the railway station and the neighborhood, setting fire to several storehouses. Seeking altitude again, Newkirk sighted a couple of armored cars below. Ordering Hank Geselbracht and Frank Lawlor to follow, Jack roared down to the attack. As they passed over the cars a sheet of flame suddenly enveloped Newkirk's plane and it crashed into the road as Geselbracht sped by. Evidently "Scarsdale Jack" had been hit by ground gun fire. Thus the Second Squadron lost its leader.

The "revenge" strafing of Chiengmai had been achieved at bitter cost. What happened to "Black Mac" McGarry the Tigers were never to learn. The Japs did not broadcast a report of his capture. Weeks later Chinese searching parties found the body of an American pilot at a point one hundred miles from where a Tomahawk had crashed. Positive identification was not possible.

With McGarry and Newkirk gone, the A.V.G. lost two of its leading aces. Each had been credited with ten and a half Jap "certains," and doubtless many more had fallen victims of their skill and daring in the Burma skies.

Long before this, "Scarsdale Jack" was a name known the length and breadth of America. The first war correspondents who came to Rangoon early in January to tell the amazing new story of the A.V.G. were not permitted to use the surnames of the pilots in their cables. The newspaper men hotly resented this censorship, arguing with complete justification that after December seventh practically everyone in the known world was well aware of the fact that Americans were waging war against the Japanese. So the journalists tried to outwit the witless censorship by using identifying nicknames for the fliers. Many of their first stories centered upon "Scarsdale Jack," who as leader of the Second Squadron commanded the aerial defense of Rangoon for the A.V.G. Thus Jack came to epitomize for the folks back home the gallantry and glory of the entire Group. When he was killed, millions of people in Britain, China and in his own land, felt the loss of Jack Newkirk in their hearts.

What kind of boy was this, who gave such great pride and such sorrow to his fellows in his few electric days?

Jack had come to the A.V.G. from the airplane carrier U.S.S. *Yorktown,* after gaining his wings at the Naval Air Training Station in Pensacola. As he read of the exploits of the R.A.F. over Britain in 1940 and 1941, he wrote his family that he longed to help "those poor kids who are doing all the dirty work." He seized the opportunity presented by Chennault's offer, and he was off for Asia and his destiny in July 1941, writing back to his bride of a few days, the former Miss Virginia Jane Dunham of Lansing, Michigan:

"This isn't going to be a vacation . . . in effect we are

going to challenge the whole aggressive movement in the Far East . . . We must set such an example with our small force that our Oriental adversary can judge the caliber of any future action our country may take."

He endured the dangers and hardships of those first days in Burma, when others resigned from the A.V.G. and returned home, because:

"I can't leave until this job is finished. There are certain things in every man's life which he cannot bear to leave undone, if he is manly. Murder and bullying of peaceful, innocent peasants is one of those things I can't stand for. Until I have done all in my power to relieve the situation I cannot leave it for the other fellow."

Miss Clare Boothe, the American playwright, visited the A.V.G. base at Kunming in April. "Scarsdale Jack," the baritone of his squadron's vocal trio "The Unholy Three," led his pals in recording some songs for Miss Boothe to take home. One of these was "Swing Low, Sweet Chariot." And Miss Boothe reported that on a subsequent visit to the hostel in Kunming, after Jack's death, she noticed that his name still marked the door of his room, and that the door was open. She asked another pilot why this was. He replied:

"Oh, we always leave it open. We have a kind of funny feeling that Jack drops in on us now and then, to see how we're doing."

On May sixteenth, Rensselaer Polytechnic Institute, which Jack Newkirk attended in 1936, conferred upon Jack, posthumously, the first alumni medal for distinguished service which the school had awarded in its one hundred and eighteen years of existence. In presenting the award to Jack's sister, Miss Janet Newkirk, and his father, Louis H. Newkirk, Dr. William Otis Hotchkiss, president of Rensselaer, said:

"To you as the sister, and to you as the father of John Van Kuren Newkirk, I cannot say more than that few will ever have so much of which to be proud. We here do not know by what philosophies he came to his decision. But we do know that while others wrangled and debated, and long before his own country was attacked, he went far away to a stricken foreign land, and there bared his stout young heart to the enemies of freedom for all men.

"He was the first American in the Burma war to be selected by the British for their Distinguished Service Order. Today Rensselaer Polytechnic Institute recognizes him as the greatest hero of all its thousands of alumni in its one hundred and eighteen years, but we have no more right to him than has the little bewildered child in Burma or elsewhere. He knew he belonged to the world, and he does. He is not dead. His spirit which flamed so fiercely in his valiant fighting lives as a torch whose glow will widen the vision of all men."

Miss Janet Newkirk, Jack's sister, received the following message on September 10, 1942:

"For all of China, we send you these few words as a token of the appreciation of the Chinese people for the invaluable service which your brother, Squadron Leader Jack Van Kuren Newkirk, rendered to the cause for which he gave his life in battle. There are no bounds of place or time to the memory of those who die for love of men. As China grieves with you in your great sorrow, she is also proud to claim a special part in preserving the record of his fair name.

Mei-ling Soong Chiang
Chiang Kai-shek"

# CHAPTER FIFTEEN

On April second, Governor Lung Yun of Yunnan Province entertained his favorite fliers at the gubernatorial mansion on a high hill overlooking the city of Kunming. The boys parked their cars near a beautiful garden, and walked along a green aisle on a carpet of pressed pine needles. Colonel Tong of the Chinese Army introduced them to the governor, once a famous war lord and foe of Chiang Kai-shek, now a fervent patriot of the new China in which he was reputedly one of the richest men. The A.V.G. was also introduced for the first time to absinthe, of the innocuous taste and the catapult effects. After the reception they entered a huge dining hall with a stage at one end, where a Chinese opera company imported from Chungking performed while the boys dealt with champagne and passed the unpopular Chinese wines through the windows to the willing hands of soldier sentries. The governor first toasted the President of the United States, and then the A.V.G. "Skip" Adair responded for the Group, representing Col. Chennault, who was in Chungking. George McMillan presented the governor with the "Flying Tiger" insignia, and made him an honorary member of the A.V.G. The combination of champagne and absinthe ambushed some of the boys late in the evening, and the governor got his first view of the American banquet sport of bread throwing. There were no casualties.

Those of the A.V.G. who had been in the Rangoon fighting luxuriated amid the pleasures of life in Kunming. They made many friends among the Chinese, and everywhere were saluted with the "thumbs up" gesture, and the call *Ding Hao*—"You are Number One." They played baseball and basketball with the Chinese, and were amazed to find, in this ancient, remote, Oriental mountain town shortstops as handy as any they had seen on the sand lots of America. They learned that ball and bat and glove had arrived with the Christian missionaries years before. On April sixth, the A.V.G. took on the Chinese in a basketball game which attracted a crowd of many thousands, and raised fifty thousand dollars Chinese for China relief. The score was China—57, America—29, the six-foot Americans having no chance against their light-footed little rivals.

Inflation and its effects proved an unending puzzle to the men of the A.V.G., confronted with the wide fluctuations in value of the Chinese dollar. When they had first come over, the exchange was eighteen Chinese for one dollar American. Although attempts were made to peg the differential around twenty for one, the return on the black market soared as high as fifty for one. Thus the boys were constantly using "telephone numbers" in their bank accounts, purchases, and the eternal games of "Red Dog" and "Acey Deucey." A big winner at these games had to have help to carry his swag to his room.

The new radios they had salvaged from the Japs at Rangoon were their principal source of entertainment in the evening. They heard American stations tell of their prowess, and listened to the popular programs they had followed at home. The Kunming movie house played fairly recent American pictures, but when the Chinese lads sought to entertain their guests with movies in the hostels, the operator was apt to run the fifth reel first and the first reel last. That made it all the better.

As the A.V.G. in Burma and China waited for new airplanes and repair of the old ones, the advancing Japs systematically blasted cities and towns of Burma in the rear of the United Nations troops, creating disorder and terror, blocking communications and lines of supply. In the first week in April, thirty-six Jap bombers devasted the ancient and storied city of Mandalay with thousands of demolition and incendiary bombs. The whole center of the city was laid waste—three thousand people killed and five thousand injured. Among those killed was Major James Wilson, who had headed the U.S. Technical Mission directing transportation over the Burma Road. Many refugees, fleeing the city hours later, were killed by exploding time bombs which had been laid along the roads. Some of the fragments were found to be from British-made explosives, presumably seized from the undestroyed stores left in Rangoon.

120

Mandalay with its scores of temples, monasteries and pagodas was a sacred city of Buddhism. It was a place of quiet and dignity, in which the traveler heard the chant of prayers, the toll of bells, and saw the shaven heads and sandaled feet of the followers of Buddha. It was no more a military objective than was Canterbury.

But the terrorism tactic was successful. Hundreds of Burmese Rifles laid down their arms and returned through the Japanese lines to their homes. Many of these were impressed into military service and forced to shower the blessings of Nipponism upon their own country and people.

With Radio Shanghai announcing complete aerial domination of Burma, the Flying Tigers of Olson's Third Squadron rose in rebuttal. At dawn on April eighth thirty Navy Zeros raced over the airdrome at Loiwing with all guns blazing. The Volunteers on the ground dove for the ditches and looked skyward, where eight of the Tigers were hidden in clouds. Down came the eight onto the backs of the Zeros. Ed Overend and Fritz Wolf got two Japs apiece in the melee, while single Zeros fell to the guns of Cliff Groh of Chicago, Arvid Olson, and Bob Little of Seattle. The eighth Jap victim was blown up by Fred Hodges of Memphis as his fiancee, Helen Anderson of Rangoon, watched from a hilltop near the field.

That afternoon the Japs came back, twenty bombers and thirty fighters strong, and they were met by Bob Brouk of Cicero, Illinois, "Buster" Keeton, Bob Smith of Los Angeles, and Bill Reed of Marion, Iowa. With bombs tearing up the field, three other Tiger planes managed to take off and join the fight above. Bill Reed, after downing a Zero, met a cross-fire from two others and had his windshield shot away. Within five minutes the Tigers sent six other Jap planes crashing in flames near the field, and the enemy started to scatter. Every A.V.G. radio then crackled with the call of Big Bob Smith:

"If none of you guys are too busy, come over here east of the river past the hill. I just got one rat and I'm busy with three others." But Big Bob had to handle this trio himself. He got one of them, his eighth of the war.

In the entire day's fighting the Tigers scored fifteen Jap "certains," and seven "probables."

Meanwhile the Chinese ground troops were trying to hold Toungoo, the old "college town" of the A.V.G.'s training days, against furious Jap attack by land and air. Without a single airplane to protect them, the Chinese battled gamely, while the unchallenged bombers showered destruction on them with a new and dreadful weapon, a fifty-pound incendiary which spattered phosphorus as it exploded. Chinese soldiers burned to death where they fought. Others stripped off their flaming khaki and fought naked under the deadly Burmese sun. Without tanks and artillery, outnumbered more than two to one, the Chinese retreated across the Sittang River.

The city of Prome also fell, after a valiant stand by the British, Indians, and Chinese. It was the same story there—no Allied aircraft.

On April twelfth, "Tex" Hill and Gil Bright of the Second Squadron ran into ten unescorted Jap bombers north of Toungoo. "Tex" got three of these and Gil shot down one "certain" and one "probable." But in this period available planes were few, all the war news was bad, and the morale of the A.V.G. suffered. Both at Loiwing and Kunming the men were on the alert from four thirty in the morning until after dark. With no outlet of action, many became discouraged, and bitter homesickness set in. Seven pilots and about twenty of the ground crew resigned or were dismissed early in April.

A new interest entered the life of the A.V.G. when the pilots sent to Africa and India to bring back thirty new P-40 E's (Kittyhawks) appeared with these long awaited ships. The P-40 E had three fifty caliber machine guns in each wing, whereas the P-40 B had two thirty calibers in each wing and two fifty calibers in the nose which shot through the prop. The Kittyhawks also had belly tanks in which five hundred pound bombs could be carried, in lieu of extra gasoline supplies. All the boys were impressed with the devastating fire power of the new ships, their improved visibility and handling qualities. Ten of them had been ferried by A.V.G. pilots from Accra, on the Gold Coast of Africa, across that continent into Egypt, and across Asia to Kunming and Loiwing. This probably marked the longest ferry trip for pursuit planes in aviation history.

A further lift to their spirits was provided by Daniel Cupid. Freddie Hodges had brought his fiancee, Helen Anderson, and her family from Rangoon up to Loiwing. Freddie and Helen decided to get married. The A.V.G. chaplain, the Rev. Paul Frillman, was in Kunming, and local clergymen and magistrates had joined the civilian evacuation of Loiwing. But despite wars, evacuations and kindred obstacles, Freddie and Helen wanted to get married right away.

An immediate discussion in the A.V.G. mess solved the problem. They decided that Loiwing needed a new mayor. "Doc" Walsh, general manager for CAMCO, was nominated and elected without opposition. His first and last official act was to solemnize the nuptials.

In April, Chennault received word in Kunming that President Roosevelt had nominated him to be a Brigadier General in the United States Army Air Forces. The "Old Man" had been retired as a Captain in 1935. Now he was suddenly offered the command of the United States Army Air Forces then forming for the defense of China. The work of the American Volunteer Group under his command must have convinced Washington of his great worth, because seldom in the history of armies have men vaulted from captaincies to become generals.

It was widely rumored that Chennault intended to refuse the appointment, preferring to stay with the Chinese Army, wherein he was already a brigadier general. It was also rumored that the A.V.G. would soon be absorbed into the United States Army Air forces. This caused great perturbation among those fliers who had been trained in the Navy, and who had a natural predilection for that branch of the service.

The uncertainty and dissensions arising in the A.V.G. reached a climax late in April when Chennault appeared in Loiwing to direct the operations of the Third Squadron, headed by Arvid Olson of Chicago. The "Old Man" was besieged by requests from Chinese commanders that the A.V.G. make frequent token demonstrations of aerial strength over their ground forces to build morale. The Tigers felt that such employment of their thin resources would be unwise, but they tried a few of these missions anyway. They ran into such overwhelming swarms of Jap planes that the Tigers held an indignation meeting and decided upon a show-down. Chennault heard them out, then proposed that instead of "demonstrating" above the Chinese Fifth and Sixth Armies, they accompany the British Blenheims on a bombing raid of the big Jap air base at Chiengmai. The R.A.F. had suggested that they rendezvous over Chiengmai at eight thirty the next morning. Frank Lawlor, "Buster" Keeton, and Henry Geselbracht, named for this mission, objected that a rendezvous with the slow Blenheims in broad daylight over Chiengmai would invite disaster.

Chennault demanded to know whether they were going to take his orders or whether they were not. Lawlor replied that they would take orders that were not "silly." Chennault then invited them to submit their resignations, and twenty-eight out of thirty-four Tigers did so in a signed document.

This was a crucial stage in the life of the A.V.G., but Chennault commanded the stage. He told them that if they followed through with their resignations and attempted to leave Loiwing they would be treated as deserters. The cold steel implication of that everyone understood. It meant that they would be shot.

The resignations were withdrawn after the "Old Man" consented to cancel any further flights for morale-building over the Chinese armies. He then appealed to the Tigers for a general burial of the hatchet, and for a revival of the old spirit of the Group.

The boys responded by asking permission to raid Chiengmai with ten pursuit planes and no bombers. The Colonel smiled and agreed. The next morning at dawn, ten Tigers from the Second and Third Squadrons swooped down at dawn on the Chiengmai field and poured ten thousand rounds of thirty and fifty caliber bullets into thirty Jap planes on the field. Every last one was destroyed.

Before the end of April the Japanese conquest of Burma was a foregone conclusion. The British destroyed the oil fields at Yenangyaung which had supplied China's military machine. Thus China had lost its fuel, as well as its lines of supply from the sea. With the new Assam highway still months from completion, the only transport possibility was by airplane from India. The failure of the mission to India headed by Sir Stafford Cripps struck another cold fear into the Allied hopes in Asia. The Japanese radio stations at Shanghai and Tokyo hailed the plight of the enemy in their usual extravagant fashion:

"The entire Japanese nation congratulates our heroic airmen on the destruction of the overwhelmingly superior numerical force of the American Volunteer Group," one announcement said. "Our heroic warhawks have destroyed two thousand A.V.G. planes. We have cleaned the sky of American, British, and Chinese military aviation."

At the time Chennault had no more than thirty airplanes fit to fly, and only thirty-four pilots in Burma. However, as always, the A.V.G. rose to refute the Jap claim of annihilation. With Ken Jernstedt and Bill Reed, Parker Dupouy went scouting for Japs over the northern Shan states, encountered fifteen Zeros, and shot down seven of them without damage to themselves. A veteran R.A.F. flier who watched them from the ground said:

"It was the finest flying I've ever seen. Those Americans are simply wizards. In a scene like a movie thriller, they sent five Jap fliers nose-diving to the earth inside five minutes."

That day word came from Kunming of Johnny Blackburn's death. This young Tiger from Amarillo, Texas, had crashed while testing his guns. He had been in only two fights—the final ones at Rangoon—but in each he had knocked out a Jap airplane.

The bad news continued with the disappearance of Cliff Groh of Chicago on a ferry trip to Loiwing.

The demolition work for the British in Burma was largely accomplished by forty-five American masters of destruction who had wrought their havoc before the advancing Japs all the way from Borneo to Burma. This American technical group left Manila when war broke out. After blasting the oil fields of Borneo and Java, they were sent to Lashio where they superintended the transport of sixty thousand tons of lend-lease material into Free China. Then they turned to their real role as "the dynamiters." Armed with matches, gasoline and dynamite, these Americans could destroy a truck in three minutes, a loaded

125

warehouse in ten minutes, and a large bridge within a quarter of an hour. Often they worked under the direct fire of Jap field pieces.

Other extraordinary services that distinguished the Burma retreat were those of the pilots of the China National Aviation Corps, the famous "CNAC," owned and operated jointly by Pan American Airways and the Chungking government. With seven battered and patched airplanes, unarmed, and under constant threat of attack, these pilots removed ten thousand refugees into India and China by the first week in May, and were still coming back for more on a constant, desperate shuttle between life and death. On their return trips they carried four to five tons of military and medical supplies for the soldiers and refugees. The country over which they flew comprised a vast, green hell of jungle with mountain peaks ten thousand feet high, but they made several trips a day, despite planes that flew lopsided with mismatched engines and mismatched wings.

A notable hero of those dark days was Dr. Gordon Seagrave of the American Baptist Mission. One month his hospital was bombed seven times. His ambulances were strafed, his supplies cut off, but he worked through the long hot days and at night under the glare of gasoline lamps to save the lives and ease the pain of hundreds of Chinese soldiers.

Most of the medical supplies of the Red Cross China Relief unit had been evacuated from Rangoon successfully. Carl R. Myers of Minneapolis, assistant director of the Red Cross unit, and a veteran of twenty-three years' work in war-torn countries, reported his experiences to the New York *Times:*

"I was a hop, skip and jump ahead of the Japs all the way all through Burma but succeeded, with the help of Dr. Robert Lim, chief of the Chinese Army Medical Corps, in getting practically every bit of medical supplies out of Burma ahead of the Japs in plenty of time," he said. "Two days before the Japs broke through to Lashio, however, several plane loads of medical supplies were flown in from India. I hurriedly rounded up some trucks and loaded these and sped northward late in the evening before the Japs came in.

"Figuring the Japs would remain in Lashio for a couple

of days' looting before pushing on, I decided to chance it and turn down toward Bhamo and evacuate fifty brand new Studebaker truck chassis, which had been shipped up the Irrawaddy from Rangoon. These were to have been assembled in Bhamo and fitted with special ambulance bodies for the Chinese Army.

"At Bhamo I discovered that owing to a shortage of labor only thirty-five trucks had been assembled and we worked forty-eight hours without a let-up making makeshift bodies with lumber from fences and doors of abandoned houses. At the last minute I gave six trucks to a Chinese officer who urgently asked for them to evacuate wounded soldiers from the Shwebo front.

"Then loaded with airplane engines, machine tools and plane parts from the CAMCO aircraft factory at near-by Loiwing, with batches of refugees riding perilously on top of the loads, we started in a blinding midnight rain over the famous one-way Bhamo road toward its junction with the Burma Road at Milepost 105 along the toughest, most treacherous road I have ever seen or hope to see again.

"We slithered along the washboard road, with fourteen hundred hairpin turns in sixty-four miles, snaking along precipitous mountain sides. That night we lost two trucks with crews who skidded off into space over a five thousand foot sheer drop.

"At Namhkam, halfway to the Burma Road junction, we learned that the Japs had already reached Kutkai. Without stopping we raced ahead to beat the Japs to the junction.

"Whenever we slowed down crowds of refugees piled on. We couldn't very well keep them off. One pregnant woman actually gave birth atop a lumbering, swaying, rain-soaked truck.

"The traffic jam along the road was so bad that on the section we moved only twelve miles in fourteen hours, due mostly to drivers who refused to stay in line. One jam was dissolved with efficiency and dispatch when an energetic Chinese officer took charge, stationing soldiers every one hundred yards with orders to shoot any driver who got out of line, after which the line moved smoothly.

"Selecting a place five miles outside Yungchang we decided to spend the night for a well-earned rest. I rounded up my remaining twenty-five trucks and had just got set for gassing and a general check-over when all of a sudden some one yelled, '*Ching pao,*' meaning 'air raid.'

· "I didn't believe it and tried to set a brave example for jittery mechanics and service men when suddenly I saw them coming. Not bravely I dove under a truck—it would be our gas truck—and watched bombs from sixty-three Japanese planes headed straight for us. I was sure we were all goners and closed my eyes with a prayer.

"The city took an awful beating from indiscriminate bombing with at least two thousand dead."

# CHAPTER SIXTEEN

The A.V.G., forced out of Loiwing when Jap bombs wrecked the CAMCO factories and air field, established its base at Paoshan, China, where the men were housed in an ancient monastery. The city was inundated by a great backwash of the Burma war. Refugees slept in the streets and during the days milled about seeking transportation into the interior.

With no warning net, the Tigers were surprised on the ground at Paoshan on May fourth by twenty-five Jap bombers. Charley Bond, newly appointed vice commander of "Adam and Eves," was the only one able to get his plane into the air. As Charley chased the bombers, he saw them sow an artistic pattern of murder on the city of Paoshan. As a second wave of thirty bombers appeared from the north, Bond attacked the rear of the right flank bomber. A couple of the others let out blue-white smoke. He knew he hadn't hit them and recognized the trick the Japs had adopted to lure the Tigers into range of their guns.

Bond concentrated on the rear bomber and on his third burst its left engine disintegrated and caught fire. The big ship went into a spin and disappeared into the overcast below. Bond suddenly realized he had chased the flight clear into Indo-China. Out of ammunition, he flew back to survey the damage at Paoshan.

As Charley himself told it:

"As I sat there fat, dumb and happy three Jap Model 'O' fighters came in above me and started shooting. I didn't even know they were there, but the boys on the field saw them. I started back to land and suddenly heard three terrific explosions. Smoke spouted from my plane. Other explosions followed. I still didn't know the Jap bullets were hitting me. As red flames hit me in the face I turned and saw the Japs on my tail. After a moment of paralysis I rolled back my canopy, rolled to the right and got ready to climb out. The ship gave a lurch and the next thing I knew

I was tumbling head over heels. I waited a second and then pulled my rip-cord. Suddenly I was head down again looking up into the cloudy sky. The parachute stretched out full length, and as it blossomed it gave me a severe jolt. I closed my eyes and hoped the enemy wouldn't strafe me. I felt severe pain suddenly in my hands and face. As I landed hard I jerked my way out of the harness and saw a Jap coming down to shoot me, but luckily Bob Little had seen him too and drove the Zero away. I hadn't even known Bob was in the air. The pain spread to my neck and shoulders so I jumped into a rice paddy and put out the fire in my clothes. I felt of my head and drew away a bloody hand. I began to feel awful pain, then I noticed a native coming for me with a huge rock in his hand. I made him understand I was 'A.V.G.' and then he took me to near-by buildings where there was a telephone. Somehow I got them to understand that I wanted to get Dr. Richard at the A.V.G. hostel.

"God! The agony I went through until he arrived. I wanted to die. I'd lie down, get up, lie down, sit down then walk back and forth holding my hands up to keep the circulation to a minimum. They took my clothes off. I was badly burned. Finally Doc Richards showed up. He greeted me as he would have a son. How good it was to see that sun-of-a-gun's mug! My head wasn't badly hurt; just a few cuts from explosive shells. But I had huge blisters all over my back and my face and hands were well scorched. Doc gave me a shot in the arm, a couple of dope capsules and then started pulling skin off the blisters. What agony! But to top that off he poured peroxide into the raw wounds. I nearly hit the ceiling and then I guess I went into some minor convulsions. But with all the pain I was glad old Doc Rich was there to help me. Then he smeared gentian violet, a purple salve, all over my body. What a mess I was! At last the dope I took, took effect and I managed to laugh.

"When we got to the field we learned poor Benny Foshee had been badly wounded in the legs by bomb splinters. A Chinese doc wanted to amputate but Benny said: 'No, get Doc Rich.' Poor Benny died before Doc could get to him. He was a Navy flier from a little town called Red Level, Alabama. We had liked Benny very much.

"The Japs had strafed the field and only Bob Little's

plane was intact. Neale and Little drove me into the city brandishing their pistols to force our way through the badly jammed road. The city was a pitiful sight. There were great holes in the ground, bombed shacks in flames, the blood-spattered faces of Chinese and some isolated legs and arms twisted in terrifying shapes. When Bob Little had to move a huge pile of timber from our path, a human head rolled out of it into the gutter. The saddest sight was one aged Chinese woman who knelt in the street crying over the body of a dead child. At the hostel Doc Rich gave me some sleeping pills and I lay down on my blistered back, thanked God I was still alive and went to sleep. The next day we took Benny's body back to Kunming. There I joined Bob Brouk in the hospital. He had been shot through the legs at Namsang by a Jap fighter. Doctor Sam Prevo covered me with more of the purple salve and the gang started calling me the minstrel man. Everyone was fine and hurray I had two letters from home."

Charley saved his Chinese parachute. Today he still wears it—to bed. It's now silk pyjamas.

Every volunteer who had occasion to test the services of the A.V.G. hospital units came forth with fervent praise of the staff. The medical unit, headed by Major T. C. Gentry, had an efficient and loyal staff consisting of Dr. Lewis Richards and Dr. Samuel Prevo, and the two nurses, Emma Jane Foster of State College, Pennsylvania, and Josephine Stewart, of Dallas, Texas. In any popularity contest of the entire Group personnel "Jo" Stewart and "Red" Foster would have been peak competitors. Both girls were tireless in their work and unending in their kindness to the injured and wounded of the A.V.G. In February, Emma Jane Foster had married John Petach, the Tiger from Perth Amboy, New Jersey, in Kunming.

The A.V.G. remained at Paoshan to assist in the defense of Yunnan Province. The Tigers kept hammering the Japs from the air as the Chinese dug in to hold to the death on the good earth. Yunnan was vitally important since it held many war production factories, and rich tin, copper, and iron mines. Its mountain ranges, slit by tempestuous rivers and almost devoid of roads, it made an ideal field for the Chinese strategy of attrition, or magnetic warfare. With the Japs beginning a new offensive in Chekiang province to the

131

east, it was essential to Chinese morale, as well as to Chinese strategy, that the Japs be held back in Yunnan. In this defense Tom Jones of Walla Walla, Washington, was a brilliant figure.

Tom was the archetype of those men of the American Volunteer Group—and they were many—who saw their service in Asia as a crusade to right some of the wrongs visited on the world by the monstrous plotters of Tokyo and Berlin.

He had enjoyed a fine American boyhood: hunting and fishing with his father, playing football for Roosevelt High School in Walla Walla, and like millions of other boys, dreaming of the day when he would make the great adventure of flight. After two years at the University of Washington, he entered the naval aviation training at Pensacola, and in 1941 he was Ensign Tom Jones of the U.S.S. *Yorktown,* on duty in Hawaiian waters. Jack Newkirk was assigned to the same aircraft carrier. When they heard of the plan for the A.V.G., they knew at once where they belonged.

On the trip over Tom, like everyone else in the A.V.G., absorbed quantities of vaccines, but the fevers and plagues of Asia hit him hard and he was invalided much of the time in Kunming.

On May first his plane was shot out of control over the jungles of Yunnan. Natives found him unconscious in the wreckage of his Kittyhawk, and carried him back to Kunming. It was the A.V.G. hospital again for Tom, and he hated it bitterly. But in a few days he was out again, clamoring for an assignment.

At the airdrome, as repairs and reconstruction went on, day and night, Chennault fired radiograms to Calcutta and Cairo and the States in a frenzied search for planes and parts, wings and tail assemblies, fuel and ammunition—and men. Fresh men and fresh machines for the fresh war, the struggle to hold south China against the triumphant conquerors of Malaya, Burma and Southeast Asia.

The Japanese were not blind to the signs of the times. If no Tigers appeared, they figured, it was because there were no more Tigers. Radio Tokyo and Radio Shanghai blithely announced the destruction of the A.V.G. for the fifth or sixth time, and the Jap forces pressed on with little or no aerial protection. They saw no need of it.

On May seventh Governor Lung Yun reported to Chennault that the Japanese Red Dragon armored division had reached the west bank of the Salween River, which runs northward into China after bisecting the Burma Road above Lashio. The Chinese had crossed the bridge with their main force, but were so closely pressed they had to dynamite the bridge before a third of their troops could reach the crossing. These were now being hunted down by the Japs, but the plight of their comrades across the river was fully as desperate. This main force of Chinese was trapped, with a high barren hill behind them that they dared not try to scale in the face of the Jap fire. They took up their stand behind their trucks, while the overwhelmingly superior Jap force filed down through the narrow gorge road opposite and prepared to blast them at leisure. The Chinese had rifles and a few machine guns, and the ineffectual cover of their trucks. The Japs had tank guns and field artillery. It was only a question of time, Governor Lung told Chennault.

"Our troops are at their mercy," Lung said. "Our own general has just killed himself in shame for the hopeless plight into which he has led his men. I am going out to take command myself. But there is only one way to stop them—from the air."

Chennault assessed the fighting strength of the A.V.G., and found it woefully low. But if that Jap Army once crossed the Salween, they would command the Burma Road, occupy the city of Paoshan, and be in position to strike at Kunming itself. This, he recognized, was a crisis. He promised the Governor immediate air assistance. How much, Chennault was ashamed to say.

David "Tex" Hill was ordered to lead a flight of four Kittyhawks, each carrying a five hundred pound bomb. The "Old Man" picked Ed Rector of Marshall, North Carolina, and Frank Lawlor of Pensacola as second and third men, and Tom Jones, the refugee from a sick bed, insisted so vehemently on being the fourth that the Colonel assented. Arriving over the Salween, they had a perfect view of the unequal battle below. The Chinese position was truly hopeless. Across the river, along a steep winding road, wound the supply train of the entire Red Dragon division. The Tigers' assignment was to blast the road and cut off this supply from the army on the river bank.

Hiss led his flight in a long half-circle to the very end of the Jap caravan. There he signaled the others, and suddenly they were driving earthward in the eight-mile-a-minute fury of the bombing dive. After they let loose their bombs they sped on over the length of the supply train, their machine guns strafing every foot of the way. The Japs scurried for shelter, and a few thuds against their fuselages reminded the Tigers that they were in a battle. Approaching the river they zoomed swiftly to clear the high east bank, and as they did they saw that the Chinese had quit fighting to conduct a disorganized but delighted cheering section of waving caps and guns below.

Surveying their work, the Tigers saw that most of the road was still intact. They went back for one more strafing, and then returned to Kunming to report to Chennault. He had four other planes ready, loaded with thirty-five pound Chinese-made bombs, and assigned Jim Howard to direct a second mission. With Jack were Frank Schiel of Prescott, Arizona, and Charles Laughlin of Ashland, Missouri. But they needed a fourth man. Who would it be? Tom Jones and his eloquence settled that.

When the trapped Chinese saw this new flight of Tigers appear over the Salween, they waved their welcome and prayed for results. They got them, speedily. The Tigers raced high above the end of the Jap train, then ran down to administer the prescribed dosage of incendiary and fragmentation bombs. The destruction they wrought was tremendous. From their "grandstand" seats the Chinese saw gasoline trucks disappear in abrupt clouds of smoke, watched trucks and tanks smashed out of control go plunging down the precipice, as the Tigers bombed and machine gunned the entire line almost to the water's edge. Back went the Tigers to repeat the operation, and as they soared again above the east bank, they saw that the entire Chinese force had forsaken applause to spring into action. They swarmed into the river, waving their rifles above their heads and heading for the Japs like men possessed. At the same time the Chinese stranded on the other side jumped from their hiding place and let loose a withering crossfire on the Japs trying to escape up the bombed road. The Tigers couldn't miss this. They flew back over the scene of the sudden wild rout, pumping their fusillades into the fleeing Japs until the road was heaped with dead amid the flaming ruins of the long military caravan. Finally, and regretfully, with ammunition exhausted and fuel going fast, they dipped their wings to the charging Chinese and returned to Kunming to report that all was well along the Salween.

The next morning they heard much news. One of their bombs had demolished the Jap field headquarters, wiping out scores of officers. The Chinese had killed over two thousand Japs and were chasing the survivors back to the frontier. The upper Burma Road and Paoshan were saved.

A week later came the accolade. From Chungking the Generalissimo wired his personal congratulations and asked for the names of the victorious pilots.

A few days later Tom Jones waited upon General Chennault. Tom had heard about some obsolete Russian bombers which the Chinese at Chungking were hoarding for an emergency. The Colonel had heard all about them, too, and the grizzled old air fighter and his young lieutenant discovered they were entertaining exactly the same thought—a big bombing expedition by the Flying Tigers. A few days later the bombers were flown down from Chungking and carefully concealed in the vicinity of the Kunming airdrome. Then Tom and the Colonel pored over maps and reports, seeking to determine where they could strike the Japs the most telling blow. Like youngsters with a set of wonderful new toys they smacked their lips over the prospect. For months and months they had longed for bombers. Now they had them, and they loved them, though they knew what clumsy, slow-moving, antiquated things they were. The question of where to take them? Tokyo? That was where they belonged, but with bitter regret they had to discard that idea. The Russian bombers had a top range of one thousand miles, and Tokyo was too far away.

So they settled for the next best choice, Hanoi in Indo-China, four hundred miles away, where the Japs had a great air base that supplied its aerial offensives out of Indo-China. Before dawn the next day Tom was off for Hanoi, with Johnny Petach, John Donovan of Montgomery,

Alabama, and three other Tigers to make a rendezvous near Hanoi with the twelve bombers and their Chinese Army pilots. They joined forces on the minute of schedule, and as the sun came up, saw forty Jap ships in neat formation on the runway, a perfect target. The Tigers leveled off well above the field and dropped their five hundred pound bombs from the belly tanks, then continued on strafing the big military establishments. Climbing away they saw columns of smoke arising from the close packed Jap formation. Then the Chinese up above let loose with their one thousand pound burdens. One of these dropped squarely in the center of the Jap formation and immediately the air was full of flying motors and wings and columns of flame and smoke. The Tigers strafed the field once more and counted thirty Jap ships far past the stage of salvage. As he climbed to get away, John Donovan was hit by antiaircraft, his plane fell out of control and he crashed in the jungle.

All others on the expedition returned to Kunming safely. When the Generalissimo received Chennault's report, he ordered the promotion of Tom Jones of Walla Walla to vice squadron commander and raised all the other Tigers one degree in rank.

Tom was the happiest boy in the A.V.G. He radioed his family the big news and made an appointment with his wife to bring their new daughter to New York to meet him on his return to the States in July. That daughter, Susan Elizabeth, had been born two months after Tom's arrival in Asia. But he was never to see Susan Elizabeth. Two days later Tom took his new Kittyhawk up to test its guns. Nearing the field, his plane fell into a ground loop and he was killed in the crash before the eyes of his comrades.

# CHAPTER SEVENTEEN

Late in May the American Volunteer Group lost two more of its best pilots. On the morning of the twenty-second Bob Little commanded a flight which included Joe Rosbert and Charley Sawyer of Emmett, Idaho, to bomb Jap artillery emplacements near Paoshan along the Salween. The Tigers went in at one thousand feet to drop their thirty-pound bombs on the target. The right wing of Little's ship was shot away by anti-aircraft fire and plummeted to earth, giving Bob no chance to bail out. A former Army pilot, from Spokane, Washington, he had been credited with ten and a half Jap ships, and so was one of the leading aces of the A.V.G.

On May twenty-eighth, Flight Leader Lewis Bishop, a fine Navy flier from Pensacola, and Col. Robert L. Scott, Jr., of the U.S. Army Air Forces, headed for Laokay in Indo-China on a strafing mission. They ran into anti-aircraft fire near the border, and Bishop had to take to his parachute. It was learned later that he had been interned by Vichy French authorities in Indo-China and turned over to the Japanese at Hanoi as a prisoner of war.

Col. Scott had arrived in April to learn the technique of downing Japanese from the A.V.G. Although he had commanded the Seventy-eighth Pursuit Squadron in Panama and was a former supervisor of Army Air Corps pilot schools in Southern California, Col. Scott "demoted" himself to the role of wing man on every A.V.G. strafing and bombing mission that came along. When the A.V.G. had no flight schedule, Scott operated as a one man air force over Burma. He won the Army Silver Star award for destroying a Japanese plane and two supply trucks near Myitkyina on May fifth. In quick succession thereafter he knocked out a Japanese anti-aircraft battery, bombed the Myitkyina air base runway three times and raided Homalin. Col. Scott was learning the ropes the hard way and everyone in the A.V.G. was delighted with him.

Chennault, given command of the U.S. Army Air Forces

operating in China, selected Scott to head his fighters—the Twenty-third U.S. Army Pursuit Group. In charge of bomber operations he had another man of his own stamp, Col. Caleb V. Haynes of Mount Airy, North Carolina, holder of many bomber speed and load records and the first man to fly a B-24 from America to Asia. The "Old Man" was pleased with these lieutenants. Now he needed men and planes to fight under them, and mechanics to keep those planes in fighting shape.

At the end of May, Lieut. Gen. Joseph W. "Vinegar Joe" Stilwell ended his famous retreat through the jungles and mountains separating Burma from India, and issued a notable statement:

"I claim we got a hell of a beating. We got run out of Burma, and it is as humiliating as hell. I think we ought to find out what caused it and go back and retake it . . . The Japanese are not supermen. If we go back properly proportioned and properly equipped, we can throw them out."

The old general, commanding a polyglot array of soldiers of three Allied armies, loyal Burmese tribesmen, and refugees of every Oriental race, had led them to safety in India through three exhausting weeks of foot travel without losing a single member of the party. In deadly heat, and chilling tropical rains, beset by snakes and wild beasts as well as dysentery, malaria, and lack of food and sleep, General Joe maneuvered the retreat. The real reasons for the collapse in Burma he told the secret war council of the United Nations in New Delhi.

As June came the men of the A.V.G. began counting the days to July fourth, the expiration date of their contracts with CAMCO to "manufacture, service and operate" airplanes in Asia. In the innumerable "bull sessions" that were their principal recreation at night they discussed what they would do when the Group passed out of existence.

They were homesick for their mothers and fathers, their friends, their girls, good American food, clean houses, big comfortable beds, and the dear familiar ways of their own country. They were deadly tired of the strains of war, of the discomforts of life in a war-torn foreign country, and their weariness showed in their gaunt faces. Most of them had suffered from malaria, dysentery, and dengue fever, and not a few had entertained Jap lead and steel in their bodies.

They had fought a good fight against tremendous odds, under unceasing difficulties, and, quite simply, they wanted a rest and a chance to play for a while.

Army officers, newly arrived in China to assist Lieut. General Joe Stilwell, presented an appeal from President Franklin D. Roosevelt to the men of the A.V.G., asking them to stay on and help train and direct the manpower of the new air force under Chennault. Some of these officers urged Chennault to use his personal influence to hold the Volunteers in China. But although he alone had to shoulder the responsibility for the new air force, the "Old Man" refused to exert pressure on the men of the A.V.G.

"They deserve to go home if they want to," he said. "Much as I regret their disbandment, I know they can stand just so much. They were the finest bunch of fighting fliers the world ever saw. I owe much to them, because they gave me the greatest opportunity any air force commander ever had—to train and direct, in complete freedom of action, a group of brave and skillful military aviators."

Some of the men could not bear to leave their leader and his fight for China which they had made their own. David "Tex" Hill, John Gil Bright, Ed Rector, and Frank Schiel appeared before the U.S. Army Induction Board at Chungking, and came out as air force majors. Charley Sawyer was made a captain. Bob Neale was offered the oak leaves of a lieutenant colonel. Six-foot Bob by this time was a potential wraith, weighing one hundred and forty-seven pounds, as against the one hundred and eighty he had carried into Burma nine months before. Nevertheless, Bob, John Petach, Bill Bartling, Charley Bond, and a few more war-worn boys told the "Old Man" that they would remain for two weeks following July fourth to help him out. And other Tigers assured the "Old Man" that they'd be back to take his orders once again after they'd gotten that cherished taste of home.

The aces of the "Adam and Eve" Squadron received the decoration of the Order of the Cloud Banner at Kunming on June sixth, together with handsome gold wings and medallions studded with stars, indicating by their number how many Jap planes the wearer had accounted for. The prized Order was also bestowed for "outstanding bravery" on Crew Chief Harry E. Fox, of Coronada, California, Radio Operator A. Mihalko, of Toledo, Ohio, and Armorer H. Pistolle of Sparton, Tennessee.

On June seventh a cadaverous, haggard-eyed individual in soiled and tattered khaki shirt and pants, sporting a long and lush brown beard populated by fleas and thorns, presented himself at the Kunming hostel with the announcement that he was Cliff Groh of Chicago and the A.V.G.

Now Cliff Groh had been missing for six weeks from a ferry flight, and given up for lost. The boys stared at this apparition and professed considerable disbelief.

"Let's get him out from behind that shrubbery," someone suggested. "Then we can tell."

"It can't be Cliff Groh," objected another Tiger. "Nobody could get that dirty and lousy in forty-three years."

Tonsorial, insecticidal, antiseptic and bathing operations followed, and there emerged the Cliff Groh they had known, twenty pounds less of him, but indubitably Cliff, with a story to tell between bites of the first square meal he had met in forty-three days.

"I got caught in a rainstorm that day in April, and lost track of the rest of the boys," he said. "We were pretty far into the hills and my gas ran out without me ever having found a single familiar landmark.

"So I looked for a flat spot and set her down. A couple of natives came along and I tried my pidgin Chinese on them. They understood me pretty well, and told me that Jap soldiers and an airdrome were close by. But they promised to protect me.

"The first thing I did was gather what dry brush I could find, and set fire to my 'Tommy.' I wasn't going to let the Japs have that. Then I offered my new pals some money to get me back to Kunming. They'd never heard of Kunming. But they didn't like Japs, and I was happy about that.

"They took me to their village, and the chief was nice to me, and promised to help me get back, after the rain stopped. He was a wise old guy, and didn't complain when I put some dough in his hand.

"After I had a little food I got out a deck of cards and started playing solitaire in the chief's hut. The chief and his boys were very much interested. They'd never seen playing

140

cards before. So I decided to teach 'em how to play 'red dog.' I had quite a time, with my pidgin Chinese and sign language.

"They didn't seem to get it at all. The next morning I wanted to get going, but no, the chief wanted to play 'red dog.' So did the assistant chief and two other guys.

"So I sat down and started my instructions all over again. But the chief waved his hands and pulled out the dough I'd given him. He was ready to play, he said. So were the rest of his boys. And by gosh, they started to 'take' me. Yes sir, they'd been setting up all night practicing 'red dog,' and they were experts already!"

The rains fell, and Cliff stayed on, playing "red dog." After three days of uninterrupted showers, Cliff sought to vary the monotony by introducing stud poker. By this time every card in the deck was as black as a spade, and Cliff was scratching himself on a twenty-four-hour basis. The rains of the monsoon continued, so did the card games, and so did the itching. Cliff didn't know whether he was fifty or five hundred miles from Kunming, but he decided to find out. He presented the deck of cards to the chief, and started off through the jungle. After weeks of wandering and privation he found his way home.

While the Second and Third Squadrons remained at Kunming to guard Yunnan and the upper Road, the "Adam and Eves" were assigned to combat the Japanese push from the vicinity of Canton into the southern provinces of China. With twelve planes and pilots they took their stand at Kweilin, where they found the best airfield they had seen in Asia. This was one of many the farsighted Generalissimo had ordered built against the day when China would have substantial air reinforcement. The Kweilin airdrome stretched a mile long, was lined by high earthworks (revetements) to protect parked planes, and surrounded by hills dotted with cone-shaped peaks of solid rock. A cave in the hillside housed the operations office and another afforded air raid shelter for thirty thousand persons. For many days before their arrival the airdrome had been bombed by wave after wave of the invader. The Tigers purposed to upset this program.

The first warning on June twelfth came at five-twenty-five a.m. Neale, Burgard and Bond immediately took off with their flights to the northwest, well out of sight of the field, and waited for the word. At nine o'clock their radios spoke: "Come on in, boys. The weather's fine."

That meant the Japs were there in force on the first routine raid of the day. The Tigers quickly found them, eleven I-97 fighters with what looked like ten bombers. The battle was joined three miles above Kweilin. In the first dive Neale, "Snuffy" Smith, Burgard and Rossi each splintered a Jap fighter in their customary fashion, but the boys who took on certain of the other Japs had a different experience, and a startling one; for five of the ten larger Jap ships were not bombers at all, but new two-engined fighters patterned exactly on Germany's famed Messerschmitt 110. These swift strong planes not only refused to crumple up in flames from the Tiger bursts, but actually got on the Tigers' tails as they roared down through the formation. The Tigers eluded them on the first dive, and, regaining altitude, avoided the big fighters to concentrate on the others. Rosbert and Prescott and Rossi scored on Jap bombers, Bartling and "Snuffy" Smith sent two I-97's spinning on their familiar course earthward. As the Tigers leveled off below, Burgard and Neale were beset by the Jap-style Messerschmitts. Neale's assailant forced him out of the fight, and George had a dogfight on his hands, through seventy-five miles of twisting, turning, and shooting, before he sent the Jap into a forced landing and crack-up. Not stopping to survey the damage, George headed back for the fight, but the eight surviving Japs had already retired to report the presence of the Flying Tigers on the southern Chinese front.

Thirteen Japs had been knocked down, but Charley Bond was missing and Pete Wright's plane had been shot down and destroyed by fire. Pete's injuries were not serious, so the fears of the "Adam and Eves" centered on Charley, whose luck had been running so badly.

Bond's guns failed to work early in the fight, just after he had crippled a bomber. Attacked by two fighters, Charley's Tomahawk engine was hit, his power left him and he nosed down expecting the worst. The Japs followed him down to eight hundred feet, and then, apparently thinking he was accounted for, leveled off and left him to crash. Charley aimed for a rice paddy, hit it at one hundred miles per hour, bounced over a dike and stopped with a terrific jolt in deep mud. Bruised and bloody from the crack-up, he retained consciousness, and clambered out of the plane just as it caught fire.

After convincing a Chinese coolie that he was not a Jap (Charley's face, burned in his May fourth crash, gave him a swarthy dark yellow appearance) the coolie led him on a three-hour trek over a mountain to the town of Yang-Tu and the Roman Catholic mission. There Charley met the Rev. Herbert Elliott, from New York City. Father Elliott treated his injuries, gave him luncheon, and then suggested a visit to the mandarin, or mayor. As they went out into the street a crowd of hundreds of Chinese greeted them with cheers and exploding firecrackers. Bond couldn't understand it.

"Why, my boy, this is the greatest moment the town has had in years," Father Elliott explained. "They know all about the wonderful exploits of the Flying Tigers and the A.V.G. here."

Two Chinese boys ran out from the crowd, came smiling up to Charley, and touched his coveralls reverently. Others surrounded him, trying to touch him, gazing at him with worshiping eyes, as their elders smiled, nodded their heads vigorously, and gave the "thumbs up" salute.

"They've been bombed for almost four years, regularly," said the priest. "Think what it means to them to see one of the famous Flying Tigers right here, fighting for their town and their homes and their children."

Charley felt like most heroes feel. He wanted to take his blushes and run away from there. At the mayor's mansion that dignitary bowed delightedly, and made a speech of greeting that brought down the house. Charley ventured a few words of response, which no one understood, including Charley. A soldier guard of honor then escorted him to the station, through ovation after ovation punctuated by blasts of firecrackers. The station master bowed low, handed him to the train, and promptly set off more firecrackers. As Charley leaned out of the window and waved good-by, a thousand of the little people of China told him from their throats and hearts that they wished him well.

The talk at the hostel that night was about Charley's mishap and subsequent triumph, and about the wonderful

143

new two-engined pseudo-Messerschmitts of the Japs, with their tremendous speed and their four fifty caliber machine guns. The crew of the one which Burgard had shot down survived the crack-up, hauled out a machine gun and were holding off Chinese soldiers seventy-five miles outside Kweilin. Burgard blamed himself for not having strafed his victims after they landed. But the Jap fliers expired that night from over-exposure to the Chinese, and the next morning other Jap planes came over the spot and set fire to the wrecked fighter.

Fresh reports of Japanese employment of mustard and lewisite gas against Chinese ground troops and civilians reached the "Adam and Eves" at Kweilin. The evidence against the Japs' inhuman warfare was incontrovertible. Not only did their planes sow gas bombs in advance of land forces, but they also scattered on Chinese towns thousands of little cotton bags filled with the germs of bubonic plague (the Black Death). When President Roosevelt issued a warning in June against continuation of these practices, the Japanese radio made answer:

"Uncle Sam's boys will soon be given a smell of their own du Pont gas which we Japanese captured at Guam."

Brig. Gen. Jimmy Doolittle and his army bombers had beaten Chennault to his cherished mission—the bombing of Tokyo—because Jimmy had the men and the planes that Claire Chennault had dreamed of for five years. But now China's grand old aerial campaigner felt that other and still grander dreams might well come true.

"Give me two hundred modern American ships, pursuits and bombers, capably manned," he said at Kweilin, "then we can defeat Japan where eventually she will have to be defeated to be turned from her mad course. Let us wipe her off the face of China; drive her armies into the sea and her planes back to her islands. With bomb and torpedo attack we can paralyze her sea lines of supply to her army and naval forces occupying Malaya, the Indies, the Philippines, and all the south Pacific. And then, when we have divorced her from her new-won empire, let us blast her industrial centers until she screams for peace. I dread the endless waste and sacrifice that must result if we try to fight Japan on a score of fronts thousands of miles away."

With the Tigers on the prowl in Kwangsi, as well as in

Yunnan Province, the effects of their presence were immediately apparent. Not once in May or June did the Japanese attempt to raid the provisional capital of Chungking, for three years before the most frequently bombed city in the world. Chinese ground forces, heartened by the sight of the famous shark-mouthed ships above them, snatched the initiative from the hated invader of their homeland, and forced back the arms of the Jap pincer in the east and south.

All China buzzed with the news of the Tiger raid on Hankow, the great interior city which had been the principal Japanese air base since its occupation in 1938.

The Tigers dropped five hundred pound bombs from the belly tanks of their Kittyhawks in a lightning visit, sinking two Jap warships and three river transports, and blowing up military establishments along the docks.

Between raids Neale, Bond, Petach and the others took the young U.S. Army pilots into the sky to teach them how to "P-forty" the Japs, while at Kunming, Older, Lawlor, Geselbracht and others of the Second and Third Squadrons trained fledgling Chinese fliers for the "Old Man's" new air force. They were counting the minutes, now, until July fourth, and so were the Japs, evidently, and understandably. The Jap fliers laid low, while Radio Shanghai and Radio Tokyo jubilantly announced that the career of the "American renegades" was nearing its end.

The end came at last, on the night of July 3, 1942. At a banquet in the mansion of the President of the Republic of China in Chungking, Generalissimo and Madame Chiang Kai-shek paid their parting tributes to the men of the American Volunteer Group.

"General Chennault and his company of air knights will always be remembered by the Chinese people as comrades in arms, and as the friendly representatives of a friendly people," the Generalissimo said. "As successors to the A.V.G. we welcome the new United States Army airmen. They no doubt will prove the same brave masters of machines in air combat. . . ."

The "Old Man" paid his tribute to his men.

"The real secret of our success was the courage and common sense of the Tigers themselves," he said.

"They did not jeopardize their lives on their equipment

145

needlessly, but when there was a fight to be fought and an objective to be gained, they gave all they had, without stint or question.

"Further, my Tigers fought not according to the book as the Japanese are trained to do, but according to the necessities of the immediate situation. They used their heads as well as their hearts. My only regret is that insufficient supplies of men and machines prevented carrying into effect our original plan of battle. That was, not merely to shoot down a few Jap planes in each formation, but at one swoop to wipe out an entire enemy formation."

The banqueteers cheered a radiogram from the States describing the entry of another Chennault into the family war against the Japanese. That day the General's son, Captain John Chennault, had led an Army Air Force attack against Jap bases in the Aleutians. The message stated:

"All the planes of Captain Chennault's unit are painted with the sign of the Flying Tigers—a symbol not exactly unknown to the enemy. Fortunately, General Chennault has a large family. Four sons are helping Uncle Sam win this war. Tokyo should be informed that our supply of Chennaults is virtually unlimited."

Toasts were drunk to Bob Neale, Charley Bond, and others of the "Adam and Eves" still fighting the war in the south, after a communique was read describing their activities. Neale, Bond, Bartling, and Petach had turned back a Jap raid on Hengyang that afternoon, destroyed six Jap ships and prevented the bombers from reaching the city and airdrome.

The question of the evening, asked innumerable times as high government officials and members of the diplomatic corps chatted with the men of the A.V.G., was: "Well, what are you going to do now?"

Twenty of the Tigers said they had contracted to fly the CNAC transport planes between India and China; a few had signed up with Pan-American, and others said they were returning to their own country to join Army and Navy forces. But most of them seemed quite unsure of the next move on their checkerboard of life. They wanted to get home, first of all. They wanted to see their folks and take their girls to dances and know the old American ways again.

As the midnight hour approached that would mark the dissolution of the A.V.G. a silence enveloped the gathering. Everyone looked at the clock. Everyone was aware that a page of history was being turned, that a great adventure was over.

The clock struck twelve. As the last note tolled, David "Tex" Hill, No. 2 ace of the American Volunteer Group, turned to his dinner partner, and said:

"Some people don't realize that we have feelings about this. When you work and fight together for a long time, you hate to split up. It's like something going out of your life."

# RECAPITULATION

The American Volunteer Group, between December 18, 1941, and July 4, 1942, was officially credited with the destruction of two hundred and eighty-six Japanese airplanes. This figure represented planes destroyed beyond the shadow of doubt, and on this figure bonuses of $500 per plane were paid to individual pilots by the Chinese Government through CAMCO, as fiscal agent.

But strewn through the jungles and mountains and waters of southeastern Asia lay undiscovered evidence of perhaps three hundred other Japanese planes that had fallen under the blows of the Tigers.

It was conservatively estimated that at least fifteen hundred Japanese airmen, pilots, navigators, gunners, and bombardiers, had lost their lives in encounters with the A.V.G.

Against these figures, the Group lost eight pilots killed in action, two pilots and one crew chief lost on the ground as the result of bombings, and four pilots missing in action, their fate unknown. Nine other A.V.G. pilots were killed accidentally, while training, in gunnery practice, or while ferrying airplanes.

At no time did the A.V.G. have more than fifty-five combat planes capable of flight, or more than seventy pilots trained to fly them. This slender strength was never concentrated at one point, but always divided between at least two bases, sometimes among three, as the exigencies of strategy dictated.

All adjectives seem pallid in relation to what these few American kids, amateurs in warfare, accomplished in the less than seven months of their service in Asia following December 7, 1941.

Beyond the chill statistics of slaughter, the record shows what the protection of the American Volunteer Group meant to the cities of China and to the transport over the Burma Road. But the true gold of their achievement lies hidden in the imponderables of the human spirit: the effect upon the long beleaguered and unaided Chinese; the inspiration to America, suddenly plunged into a worldwide war; and the knowledge driven home to the Japanese and the Germans that the men of the A.V.G. were just "floor samples" of ten million others of the same cut of jib.

Leading A.V.G. aces and the individual victories officially credited to them were:

Robert H. Neale, 16; David "Tex" Hill, 12 1/4; William Reed, 11; George T. Burgard, 10 3/4; William D. McGarry, 10 1/2; Kenneth A. Jernstedt, 10 1/2; John Van Kuren Newkirk, 10 1/2; Robert L. Little, 10 1/2; Charles H. Older, 10 1/4; Robert T. Smith, 9; Charles R. Bond, 9.

Other high ranking aces were Frank Lawlor, William E. Bartling, Robert "Duke" Hedman, Parker Dupouy, John "Dick" Rossi, Thomas Haywood, Robert J. Sandell, Robert "Snuffy" Smith, John E. Petach, James R. Howard, Joseph Rosbert, Ed Rector, John "Gil" Bright, Noel R. Bacon, George McMillan, Louis Hoffman, Ed Overend, and Fritz Wolf.

Thirty-three A.V.G. pilots were awarded the Chinese Order of the Cloud Banner for outstanding bravery and achievement in combat.

The Flying Tigers sometimes divided their $500 bonuses two, three, or four ways when in the confusion of combat it could not be accurately determined which one was responsible for bringing down an enemy plane.

## A.V.G. KILLED IN ACTION

| Name | Previous Service | Date Killed | Locality |
|---|---|---|---|
| Henry C. Gilbert, Jr. | Navy | 12/23/41 | Rangoon |
| | *Home:* Lovell, Wyoming | | |
| Neil G. Martin | Army | 12/23/41 | Rangoon |
| | *Home:* Texarkana, Arkansas | | |
| Allen Bert Christman | Navy | 1/23/42 | Rangoon |
| | *Home:* Fort Collins, Colorado | | |

| *Name* | *Previous Service* | *Date Killed* | *Locality* |
|---|---|---|---|
| Louis Hoffman | Navy | 1/26/42 | Rangoon |
| *Home:* San Diego, California | | | |
| Thomas J. Cole, Jr. | Navy | 1/30/42 | Moulmein |
| *Home:* Clayton, Missouri | | | |
| John Van Kuren Newkirk | Navy | 3/24/42 | Chiengmai |
| *Home:* Lansing, Michigan | | | |
| Ben C. Foshee | Navy | 5/4/42 | Paoshan |
| *Home:* Red Level, Alabama | | | |
| John T. Donovan | Navy | 5/12/42 | Hanoi |
| *Home:* Montgomery, Alabama | | | |
| Robert L. Little | Army | 5/22/42 | Yunnan |
| *Home:* Spokane, Washington | | | |

Two pilots and one crew chief met death on the ground as the result of Jap bombings. Frank W. Swartz, a former Navy flier from Dunmore, Pennsylvania, and John E. Fauth, former staff sergeant in the U.S. Army, an A.V.G. crew chief, died from wounds received in the bombing of Magwe on April twenty-fourth. Ben C. Foshee, a former Navy flier from Red Level, Aabama, was fatally wounded in the bombing of Paoshan on May fourth.

## KILLED IN ACCIDENTS

| Name | Previous Service | Date Killed | Locality |
|------|------------------|-------------|----------|
| John D. Armstrong | Navy | 9/8/41 | Toungoo |
| | Home: Hutchinson, Kansas | | |
| Maax C. Hammer | Army | 9/22/41 | Rangoon |
| | Home: Cairo, Illinois | | |
| Peter W. Atkinson | Army | 10/25/41 | Rangoon |
| | Home: Martinsburg, W. Va. | | |
| Lacey Mangleburg | Army | 12/24/41 | Yunnan |
| | Home: Athens, Georgia | | |
| Marion F. Baugh | Army | 1/3/42 | Kunming |
| | Home: Beverly Hills, California | | |
| Kenneth T. Merritt | Army | 1/8/42 | Rangoon |
| | Home: Arlington, Texas | | |
| Robert J. Sandell | Army | 2/7/42 | Rangoon |
| | Home: San Antonio, Texas | | |
| John E. Blackburn III | Army | 4/28/42 | Kunming |
| | Home: Amarillo, Texas | | |
| Thomas A. Jones, Jr. | Navy | 5/16/42 | Kunming |
| | Home: Lovell, Wyoming | | |

# MISSING IN ACTION

CHARLES MOTT, former Navy pilot, January 8, 1942, in Indo-China.

EDWARD J. LIEBOLT, former Army pilot, February 26, 1942, near Rangoon.

WILLIAM D. MCGARRY, former Army pilot, March 24, 1942, in Indo-China.

LEWIS S. BISHOP, former Navy pilot, May 28, 1942, interned in Indo-China.

NOTE: JOHN E. PETACH, an A.V.G. ace, was killed when his plane exploded in mid-air on July 10, 1942, in Kwangsi Province. Petach was one of those Tigers who served an extra two weeks following the dissolution of the Group on July fourth. He was the husband of Emma Jane Foster, one of the two A.V.G. nurses. The young widow returned to her parents' home in State College, Pennsylvania, in August.

# HEADQUARTERS AMERICAN VOLUNTEER GROUP

### Office of the Commanding Officer
Point "X," China.

MEMORANDUM:

TO: All Squadrons and Departments.

1. The following is a list of the Group Staff Officers and Pilots of the American Volunteer Group, showing duty assignments:

## GROUP HEADQUARTERS SECTION

| | |
|---|---|
| Chennault, C. L. | Group Commander |
| Adair, C. B. | Chief G-4 Section |
| Alsop, J. L., Jr. | Staff Secretary (DS-Manila) |
| Blackburn, J. E., III | Asst. Gp. Opns. Officer |
| Bruce, E. W. | Dental Surgeon |
| Davis, W. H. S. | Det. Supply Officer Point "A" |
| Foster, Miss E. J. | Nurse (Female) |
| Frillmann, P. W. | Chaplain Interpreter, Recreation O., Group Mess O., Liaison O., WASC, O in C. Sales Stores |
| Gentry, T. C. | Chief Surgeon |
| Goyette, E. T. | Det. Commander, Point "A" |
| Greenlaw, H. K. | Chief of Staff, Gp. Executive O, Gp. Operations O. |
| Greenlaw, O. S. (Mrs.) | War Diary Statistician |
| Harris, D. H. | Liaison O., Loiwing |
| Lee, J. | Surgeon |
| Peret, R. C. | Gp. Engineering O., Gp. Parachute O., Gp. Surveying O. |
| Prevo, S. B. | Surgeon DS Rangoon |
| Richards, L. J. | Surgeon |
| Smith, C. E. Jr. | Group Adjutant |
| Whitehead, R. W. | Asst. Gp. Operations O. |
| Williams, J. M. | Group Communications O., Asst. Gp. Intelligence O. |
| Wyke, W. R. | Asst. Group Adjutant |
| Stewart, Miss J. B. | Nurse (Female) |

| | |
|---|---|
| Bartling, W. E. | Wing Man, DS Rangoon |
| Bond, C. R. | Flight Leader, DS Rangoon |
| Boyington, G. | Flight Leader, DS Rangoon |
| Brown, C. | Wing Man, DS Rangoon |
| Burgard, G. T. | Wing Man, DS Rangoon |
| Conant, E. S. | Wing Man, Gp. Transportation O. Asst. Gp. Supply Officer |
| Croft, J. S. | Wing Man, DS Rangoon |
| Cross, J. D. | Wing Man |
| Dean, J. J. | Wing Man, DS Rangoon |
| Farrell, J. W. | Wing Man |
| Hennessy, J. J. | Wing Man |
| Kuykendall, M. W. | Flight Leader, DS Rangoon |
| Leibolt, E. J. | Flight Leader |
| Little, R. L. | Flight Leader, DS Rangoon |
| McGarry, W. D. | Wing Man, DS Rangoon |
| Mickelson, E. I. | Wing Man |
| Neale, R. H. | Vice Squadron Leader, DS Rangoon |
| Prescott, R. W. | Wing Man, DS Rangoon |
| Probst, A. E. | Flight Leader, DS Rangoon |
| Rosbert, R. J. | Wing Man |
| Rossi, J. R. | Wing Man, DS Rangoon |
| Sandell, R. J. | Squadron Leader, DS Rangoon |
| Sawyer, C. W. | Flight Leader, DS Rangoon, Liaison O., RAF Atchd. Gp. Hq. Sec. |
| Schiel, F. Jr. | Flight Leader, DS Rangoon |
| Smith, R. H. | Wing Man, DS Rangoon |
| Wolf, F. E. | Flight Leader, Acting Squadron Leader |

## SECOND PURSUIT SQUADRON
### *Command Post Rangoon, Burma*

| | |
|---|---|
| Bacon, N. R. | Flight Leader |
| Bartelt, Percy | Flight Leader |
| Bright, J. G. | Flight Leader |
| Fish, W. H. | Wing Man |
| Geselbracht, H. M. Jr. | Wing Man |
| Gilbert, Henry C., Jr. | Wing Man |
| Hill, D. L. | Flight Leader |
| Howard, J. H. | Vice Squadron Leader |
| Hurst, L. A. | Wing Man |
| Jones, T. A. | Flight Leader, Atchd. Gp. Hq. Sec. |
| Keeton, R. B. | Wing Man, DS Point "A" |

Lawlor, F.                    Wing Man
Layher, R. F.                 Wing Man
Martin, Neil G.               Wing Man
Moss, R. C.                   Wing Man, Atchd. Gp. Hq. Sec.
Mott, C. D.                   Flight Leader, missing in action
Newkirk, J. V.                Squadron Leader
Paxton, G. L.                 Wing Man, Atchd. Gp. Hq. Sec., Group
                                Finance Officer
Petach, J. E. Jr.            Flight Leader, Atchd. Gp. Hq. Sec.
Rector, E. G.                 Flight Leader
Ricketts, F. I.               Wing Man
Swartz, F. W.                 Wing Man
Wright, P.                    Wing Man, Atchd. Gp. Hq. Sec.

## THIRD PURSUIT SQUADRON

Adkins, F. W.                 Wing Man
Bishop, L. S.                 Flight Leader
Brouk, R. R.                  Flight Leader
Cavanah, H. R.                Wing Man
Donovan, J. T.                Wing Man
Dupouy, P. S.                 Flight Leader
Foshee, B. C.                 Wing Man
Greene, P. J.                 Wing Man
Groh, C. G.                   Wing Man
Haywood, T. C. Jr.           Flight Leader
Hedman, R. P.                 Flight Leader
Hodges, F. S.                 Wing Man
Jernstedt, K. A.              Flight Leader
Laughlin, C. H.               Wing Man
McMillan, G. B.               Vice Squadron Leader
Older, C. N.                  Flight Leader
Olson, A. E. Jr.             Squadron Leader
Overend, E. F.                Wing Man
Raines, E. J.                 Wing Man
Reed, W. N.                   Flight Leader
Shilling, E. E.               Wing Man, Group Photo Officer
Smith, R. T.                  Flight Leader

# HEADQUARTERS AMERICAN VOLUNTEER GROUP

### Office of the Commanding Officer

Kunming, China.

## MEMORANDUM:

## TO: All Squadrons and Departments.

1. The following is a list of the Ground Personnel of the American Volunteer Group, showing duty assignments:

### GROUP HEADQUARTERS SECTION

**GROUP COMMANDERS OFFICE:**

| | |
|---|---|
| Trumble, T. C. | Secretary to Group Commander |

**GROUP PERSONNEL OFFICE:**

| | |
|---|---|
| Breeden, K. V. | Clerk Administration |
| Fobes, E. L. | Clerk Administration |
| Harris, E. J. | Clerk Administration |

**GROUP SUPPLY SECTION:**

| | |
|---|---|
| Bell, D. | Clerk Supply & Transportation |
| Brady, J. E. | Clerk Supply & Transportation |
| Heller, J. E. | Clerk Supply & Transportation DS Point "A" |
| McHenry, S. L. | Clerk Supply & Transportation |

**TRANSPORTATION SECTION:**

| | |
|---|---|
| Allard, J. L. | Auto Mechanic |
| Beaupre, L. A. | Clerk Supply & Transportation |
| Jaeger, G. B. | Auto Mechanic DS Point "A" |
| Sutherland, W. L. | Auto Mechanic |
| Wakefield, M. Jr. | Auto Mechanic DS Point "A" |
| Wilson, C. W. | Auto Mechanic |
| Young, J. P. | Clerk Engineering |

**FINANCE OFFICE:**

| | |
|---|---|
| Jordon, J. T. | Clerk Finance DS Point "A" |
| Wylie, H. G. | Clerk Finance |

MESS SECTION:

| | |
|---|---|
| Harpold, C. K. | Mess Supervisor Hostel 2 |
| Rasbury, J. | Mess Supervisor Hostel 1 |
| Towery, W. H. | Manager Sales Stores |

GROUP OPERATIONS SECTION:

| | |
|---|---|
| Ceder, M. E. | Clerk Intelligence |
| Crotty, J. D. | Clerk Operations |
| Cushing, A. D. | Clerk Operations |
| Jourdan, W. C. | Clerk Meteorology, DS Enroute Pt. "X" |
| Lancaster, G. R. | Clerk Meteorology |
| Moss, K. R. | Clerk Meteorology |
| Richardson, R. S. | Clerk Meteorology |
| Sommers, J. T. | Clerk Operations |

GROUP ENGINEERING SECTION:

| | |
|---|---|
| Gasdick, J. | Sheet Metal Worker |
| Gee, C. Y. | Engineering Helper |
| Hooker, B. L. | Parachute Rigger, DS Point "A" |
| Janski, E. A. | Prop Specialist DS Point "A" |
| Leaghty, C. C. | Parachute Rigger |
| Lee, P. O. | Engineering Helper |
| Locke, R. P. | Prop Specialist |
| McDowell, M. H. | Line Chief |
| Pan, K. J. | Engineering Helper |
| Ricks, W. W. | Prop Specialist |
| Rogers, R. W. | Crew Chief (Beechcraft) |
| Shields, M. R. | Prop Specialist |
| Walters, G. F. | Clerk Administration |
| Wing Shee, G. L. | Engineering Helper |
| Wu, L. F. | Engineering Helper |

GROUP COMMUNICATIONS SECTION:

| | |
|---|---|
| Baughman, E. G. | Communications |
| Bonham, E. O. | Communications DS Yunnan Yi |
| Cross, H. G. | Communications |
| Doran, F. R. | Clerk Administration |
| Ernst, R. J. | Communications DS Iliang |
| Kelly, T. D. | Clerk Administration |
| Kiner, M. W. | Clerk Intelligence |
| Lindstedt, R. K. | Communications DS Lotze |
| Miller, A. A. | Communications DS Paoshan |
| Newell, F. E. | Clerk Administration |
| Richardson, R. L. | Communications DS Kunyang |
| Sasser, R. W. | Communications DS Mengtze |
| Seamster, L. F. | Communications |
| Seavey, E. H. | Clerk Operations DS Yunnan Yi |

| | |
|---|---|
| Shreffler, R. | Communications DS Chang Yi |
| Smith, R. M. | Communications |
| Sykes, W. A. | Communications DS Point "A" |
| Vaux, M. H. | Communications |
| Whelpley, D. A. | Clerk Meteorology, DS Mengtze |

GROUP MEDICAL DEPARTMENT:

| | |
|---|---|
| Buxton, R. H. | Clerk Medical Orderly |
| Cribbs, C. D. | Clerk Medical Orderly DS Point "A" |
| Gallagher, R. | Nurse (Male) |
| Henson, T. M. | Clerk Medical Orderly |
| Shaw, J. E. | Clerk Medical Orderly |
| Viverette, H. J. | Clerk Medical Orderly |

INTELLIGENCE SECTION:

| | |
|---|---|
| Durall, E. C. | Clerk Intelligence |
| Hubler, M. L. | Clerk Operations |

PHOTO SECTION:

| | |
|---|---|
| Pietsker, J. H. | Photographer |
| Regis, J. E. | Photographer |

ARMAMENT SECTION:

| | |
|---|---|
| Hoffman, R. G. | Armorer |

A. & R. SECTION:

| | |
|---|---|
| Dudzik, F. P. | Clerk Administration |

FIRST PURSUIT SQUADRON

| | |
|---|---|
| Blackburn, W. J. | Crew Chief DS Point "A" |
| Callan, M. | Crew Chief |
| Cornelius, J. | Crew Chief |
| Curran, G. F. | Crew Chief |
| Dolan, W. J. | Crew Chief |
| Dorris, C. E. | Clerk Operations |
| Gove, L. P. Jr. | Crew Chief DS Rangoon |
| Graham, R. E. | Line Chief DS Rangoon |
| Hardesty, M. L. | Crew Chief |
| Harrington, J. J. | Crew Chief |
| Jacobson, F. A. | Crew Chief DS Mengtze (Det. C. O.) |
| Jones, Jack D. | Armorer |
| Kaelin, A. V. | Clerk Administration |
| Kemph, M. D. | Crew Chief |
| Kenner, C. D. | Crew Chief |
| Kustay, S. | Armorer |

| | |
|---|---|
| Linton, J. R. | Armorer |
| Lussier, J. E. | Communications |
| McClure, E. B. | Crew Chief DS Rangoon |
| McKinney, E. R. | Armorer |
| Meisenheimer, C. V. | Crew Chief |
| Metasavage, F. G. | Crew Chief DS Mengtze |
| Musgrove, W. L. | Crew Chief |
| Neal, R. J. | Armorer |
| Rasmussen, R. P. | Crew Chief |
| Reynolds, G. B. | Crew Chief |
| Rodewald, D. L. | Armorer |
| Schaper, W. E. | Crew Chief DS Rangoon |
| Uebele, J. J. | Crew Chief DS Rangoon |
| Unger, W. H. | Armorer DS Point "A" |
| Wyatt, L. G. | Communications |
| Yarberry, G. L. | Crew Chief |

## SECOND PURSUIT SQUADRON

| | |
|---|---|
| Baileym, G. R. | Crew Chief DS Rangoon |
| Bent, M. W. | Clerk Operations DS Rangoon |
| Blackwell, H. J. | Crew Chief DS Rangoon |
| Brice, G. | Crew Chief DS Rangoon |
| Bugler, C. F. | Chief Administration DS Rangoon |
| Carter, J. B. | Crew Chief DS Rangoon |
| Chaney, C. | Crew Chief DS Rangoon |
| Daube, O. W. | Crew Chief DS Rangoon |
| Fox, H. E. | Line Chief, DS Rangoon |
| Fritzke, A. W. | Clerk Meteorology DS Rangoon |
| Gorham, L. L. | Crew Chief DS Rangoon |
| Hauser, J. B. | Crew Chief DS Rangoon |
| King, R. J. | Communications DS Rangoon |
| Mihalko, A. | Communications DS Rangoon |
| Musick, J. H. | Armorer DS Rangoon |
| Overley, J. L. | Crew Chief DS Rangoon |
| Paull, P. B. | Crew Chief DS Rangoon |
| Peeden, J. B. | Crew Chief DS Rangoon |
| Pistole, H. | Armorer DS Rangoon |
| Power, J. D. | Crew Chief DS Rangoon |
| Quick, C. | Crew Chief DS Rangoon |
| Richardson, C. A. | Crew Chief DS Rangoon |
| Roberts, C. M. | Communications DS Rangoon |
| Rumen, J. M. | Armorer DS Point "A" |
| Schiller, R. W. | Armorer, DS Rangoon |
| Tuley, C. A. | Crew Chief DS Rangoon |

Tyrrell, G. J.         Crew Chief DS Rangoon
Wagner, E.         Armorer DS Rangoon
Walker, H. H.       Crew Chief DS Point "A"
Wirta, H. C.        Armorer, Atchd. Gp. Hq. Sec.
White, J. E.        Crew Chief DS Rangoon
Woodward, M. E.    Crew Chief DS Rangoon

## THIRD PURSUIT SQUADRON

Baisden, C. N.       Armorer
Blaylock, G. O.     Line Chief
Christensen, K. J.    Armorer
Clouthier, L. P.     Clerk Operations
Colquette, L. P.     Crew Chief
Crookshanks, J. R.   Crew Chief
Engle, C. R.        Crew Chief
Fauth, J. E.        Crew Chief
Francisco, C. H.    Communications
Gallagher, E. F.    Crew Chief
Hanley, L. D.      Armorer DS Rangoon
Hoyle, D. J.       Chief Administration
Keller, D. H.      Crew Chief DS Point "A"
Kepka, G. B.       Crew Chief DS Point "A"
Loomis, E. V.      Communications
Losonsky, F. S.     Crew Chief
McAllister, G. E.    Crew Chief DS Rangoon
Mundelin, G., Jr.    Crew Chief
Olson, H. L.       Crew Chief (leave Calcutta)
Osborne, H. L.     Crew Chief
Perry, P. J.        Armorer
Poshefko, J. A.     Armorer
Regis, S. J.        Crew Chief
Riffer, C. W.       Armorer
Schramm, J. L.     Crew Chief
Seiple, W. R.      Crew Chief
Smith, R. A.       Crew Chief
Stolet, I. J.        Crew Chief
Terry, J. F.        Clerk Administration
Van Timmeren, F. A.  Crew Chief

## WORLD WAR II'S MOST HEROIC TRUE COMBAT STORY—*THE FLYING TIGERS*

General Claire Chennault's "Flying Tigers," 70 American fliers with no more than 55 planes, shot down 286 Japanese aircraft. The Japanese lost 1500 fliers—the Americans only eight.

Here is the true, inside story of the men of the American Volunteer Group who blasted the Imperial Japanese Air Force out of the sky and held open the Burma Road for months after it had been given up for lost.

"The United Nations were fortunate to have this tiny group in Rangoon when the Japanese hit Pearl Harbor, and the A.V.G. itself can count itself fortunate to have Mr. Whelan for Boswell."

*(New York Times)*

# The Flying Tigers

The Story of the

American Volunteer Group

by Russell Whelan

WARNER

®

PAPERBACK LIBRARY
NEW YORK

WARNER PAPERBACK LIBRARY EDITION
First Printing: July, 1968
Second Printing: November, 1972

This Warner Paperback Library Edition is published
by arrangement with The Viking Press, Inc.

Warner Paperback Library is a division of Warner Books,
Inc., 315 Park Avenue South, New York, N.Y. 10010.